What if it happens in my classroom?

Why can't I stop my students from being noisy as they leave my classroom? What can I do when a student is texting on their phone in my lesson? How can I stop a student from constantly tapping their pen while I am talking?

Sound familiar?

Chewing gum, dropping litter, swearing, late homework and disruptive behaviour in class are just a few of the issues that teachers have to face every day in the classroom. How you choose to respond to these incidents, however minor they may first seem, can have a dramatic impact on the overall quality of your lessons. There is no one answer to behaviour and classroom management as different approaches have to be taken depending on the lesson, the groups of students and even the time of day.

This highly practical book guides you through the choices that you need to make when confronted with the sorts of issues that you might face in your classroom. Dealing with the nitty gritty reality of behaviour management, it covers the common problems teachers encounter on a day-to-day basis and provides a series of realistic and practical solutions and their likely outcomes. Placing you at the centre of the decision-making process, it allows you to experiment with a range of options in a reflective and engaging manner to see which of your choices may work and why others may not. This scenario-based approach not only lets you explore the various options available to you, but also enables you to see the consequence of your actions.

Written by an experienced teacher, this fun and interactive book is essential reading for all trainee and qualified teachers who want a fresh approach to behaviour management in their classrooms.

Kate Sida-Nicholls has been a teacher for 15 years and currently teaches English Language at Suffolk One, a post-16 Centre. She is a trainer for the Norfolk and Suffolk ITT training programmes for Primary and Secondary teachers. She is a Lead Practitioner for English in Suffolk as well as being a member of the management team for the local SCITT programme.

What if it happens in my classroom?

Developing skills for expert behaviour management

Kate Sida-Nicholls

Routledge
Taylor & Francis Group

LONDON AND NEW YORK

First published 2012
by Routledge
2 Park Square, Milton Park, Abingdon, Oxon OX14 4RN

Simultaneously published in the USA and Canada
by Routledge
711 Third Avenue, New York, NY 10017

Routledge is an imprint of the Taylor & Francis Group, an informa business

British Library Cataloguing in Publication Data
A catalogue record for this book is available from the British Library

Library of Congress Cataloging in Publication Data
Sida-Nicholls, Kate.
 What if it happens in my classroom?: developing skills for expert behaviour
 management/Kate Sida-Nicholls.
 p. cm.
 1. Classroom management. 2. Behavior modification. 3. Problem children—
 Behavior modification. 4. School discipline. I. Title.
 LB3013.S57 2012
 371.102′4--dc23   2011048102

ISBN: 978-0-415-68713-3 (hbk)
ISBN: 978-0-415-68714-0 (pbk)
ISBN: 978-0-203-69494-7 (ebk)

Typeset in Helvetica
by Florence Production Ltd, Stoodleigh, Devon

MIX
Paper from
responsible sources
FSC
www.fsc.org FSC® C004839

Printed and bound in Great Britain by
TJ International Ltd, Padstow, Cornwall

Contents

Acknowledgements

Thanks to my colleagues in the Humanities team at Suffolk One who between them generated lots of ideas to use in this book.

Thanks to my special teacher friends – Andrea and Maeve – who gave me honest feedback and guidance.

Thank you to my family, who offered me support and encouragement but especially to Michael and Henry who also gave me the time to write this book.

Introduction

There is currently a national focus on the behaviour of students in schools which is reflected in the new Ofsted framework. Ofsted wish to see students who have 'very high levels of engagement, courtesy, collaboration and cooperation in and out of lessons. They have excellent, enthusiastic attitudes to learning, enabling lessons to proceed without interruption.' These features of outstanding behaviour (according to Ofsted) place the emphasis firmly on the teacher managing the behaviour of students within their own classroom.

There is no doubt that as teachers we would love to consistently teach every one of our lessons without interruptions from poor behaviour. However, we have all experienced the miscreant student who is determined to 'roadrail' our lesson or faced a group of students on a Friday afternoon who ignore any lesson activity that is presented to them. These types of situations can appear worse when you don't have the knowledge to deal with them. Experience can show you how to deal with the different situations that you face in the classroom as you can think back to successful strategies that you have used before and become more confident about using them. However, how do you gain that experience? Through trial and error and facing situations that you wish you had not created?

My experiences as a teacher, but also working closely with trainee teachers, have shown me that there is no one way to address poor behaviour. A successful strategy can depend on so many other factors such as time of day, the topic of the lesson or the lesson that the students have just come from. When I speak to trainee teachers about dealing with the bad behaviour of their students and suggest possible solutions, they always ask follow up questions starting 'what if . . .?'. This is what gave me the idea for this book. I wanted to demonstrate the various ways that some of the more typical and low-level behaviour issues can be dealt with in the classroom.

The book includes a range of scenarios from what to do if a student refuses to work with their teaching assistant or what to do with a student who is constantly tapping their pen while a teacher is talking. I have outlined three strategies for each issue; some are more non-confrontational than others. In each case there should be at least one option that can be tried within a classroom but I have included extra notes where I think the choices will depend on the context of the school. I have tried to write the strategies by using rhetorical questions as I wanted to capture the tone that a mentor might use to encourage a trainee to reflect on the reasons why there was poor behaviour in their lesson. The intention behind outlining three strategies for each scenario was to identify the possible outcomes of taking certain actions with students. It can be difficult in the 'heat of the moment' to anticipate what will happen next but I am hoping that this book will allow teachers to see the impact that certain actions will have on students.

In my experience, trainees will often adopt strategies that they see more experienced teachers use and are very surprised when they don't work. I have tried to emphasise in this book how developing status and the respect of the students is part of being able to maintain successful behaviour management in the classroom. This is why I included a section about 'behaviour in the corridor', as being seen to ignore poor behaviour in the corridor can have an impact on how students perceive you as their teacher in the classroom. Students have to believe that you will be a teacher who will 'follow through' no matter what. This is why it is essential to make your sanctions obtainable and realistic. For example, telling a class during the last lesson of the day that you are going to keep them all behind for a detention is not a sanction that you can easily implement without repercussions. However, if no one has told you what some possible sanctions might be for a certain situation then it can be difficult to choose the right one. This is why I thought it was important for the book to show you three different scenarios as this can help you to decide which one might be the most appropriate for the situation that you have found yourself in.

Trainee teachers always ask me what is the one behaviour strategy that I think is the most effective. Many of them have been covered in various ways by other books on behaviour: seating plans; pace of activities; clear and consistent sanctions; use of praise etc. However, I think the one that is not mentioned enough is the quantity of teacher talk. Too much teacher talk is inextricably linked to signs of poor behaviour in classrooms. Inexperienced teachers talk too much as they forget that there are other ways of explaining tasks or putting across information. One of the most effective behaviour management tools a teacher can use is not to talk for more than ten minutes before allowing the students to do some kind of activity. However, the best example is to explain to the students how long you are going to talk for and keep to it. If a student cannot behave while you are talking for the specified time then it is probably best to start some clear sanctions as soon as possible. The key is to be consistent. If you say you are only going to talk for eight minutes then only talk for eight minutes. Think about how many times students are 'talked at' during a typical school day and ask yourself how many times are they told how long this being 'talked at' is going to last? As an adult, we find being 'talked at' for long periods of time in meetings, conferences etc. extremely boring, especially if we don't know how long it is going to last. Therefore, it is likely that a group of teenagers are also going to react negatively to an adult 'talking at' them for a longer time than their attention span can cope with. Just think about that when you are standing and talking in front of your class tomorrow – how can you lessen the time that you spend 'talking at' your students?

I hope that reading this book will help you with facing the ups and downs of a teacher's journey in the classroom. It doesn't have all the answers but it might give you some strategies for the 'What if' moments that we all face on a daily basis in our classrooms.

Kate Sida-Nicholls currently teaches three days a week at a post-16 centre in Ipswich, Suffolk. Previously, she was head of an English Department at a school in Bury St Edmunds, Suffolk. She works two days a week as consultant for the SCITT teacher training programme in Suffolk and Norfolk. She also conducts training sessions on various aspects of teaching and learning for other organisations.

CHAPTER 1

MANAGING THE BEHAVIOUR OF STUDENTS AT THE START OF YOUR LESSON

What do you do when a student . . .

A bright student says your lesson is boring

A bright student (A) in your class sits down at the start of your lesson and says loudly 'This lesson is boring. We always end up doing the same thing. Why are your lessons so boring?'

HOW DO YOU HANDLE THIS SITUATION?

1 Ignore student A and carry on with the rest of the lesson and introduce the activities etc. However, student A is likely to repeat their comment at some further point in the lesson as they clearly want to send a message to you and will not stop until you have acknowledged it in some way. You will need to decide when you are going to talk to student A about their attitude and behaviour either at some stage in the lesson or after the lesson. However, you do need to address the situation as the type of attitude shown by student A can quickly spread to other students.

2 Make a sarcastic comment such as 'Thank you for your positive contribution to this lesson [name of student], I see that you are going to be making your usual perceptive comments on my lesson.' You can then carry on introducing the rest of the activities for the lesson. You will probably have defused the situation for that moment but there is the risk that student A is likely to repeat their comment at another point in the lesson in order to cause maximum impact.

3 You can do a combination of (1) and (2) beforehand but you are going to have to talk to student A at some point during the lesson. The student is trying to send you a message and you need to find out what the problem is before student A decides to become too disruptive and lead the way for others to become disruptive too.

Hopefully student A has decided to cooperate with the initial activities of the lesson; if they look as if they are not going to do this then tell them that you would like them to complete the activity and you will come and talk to them within the first ten minutes of the lesson. Try and have this initial exchange with student A on a one-to-one at their desk rather than with you saying this from the front of the classroom.

Depending on your knowledge of student A, you may wish to have this conversation with them outside the classroom but removing yourself from the room can have a detrimental effect on the learning of the others in the classroom. If you think that the conversation is going to be volatile and possibly negative then you may wish to suggest to student A that you should talk at the end of the lesson.

You may find that giving student A a piece of paper at this point and asking them to write down four points that they wish to discuss with you at the end of the lesson can 'take the wind out of their sails' slightly. You can tell student A that you would like them to set the agenda for the meeting since they clearly felt strongly enough to announce their feelings at the start of the lesson. Insist that they write four points down – no fewer. Sometimes, the thought of staying behind at the end of the lesson and also being asked to write this number of points down can make the student decide that they don't wish to meet you. You can then ensure their cooperation in the future by referring to this missed opportunity.

However, allowing student A the opportunity to write down their points makes them realise that you are taking it seriously; it will make the student think about their points rather than just use the meeting as an excuse to criticise, in a reactive manner, the activities in the lesson; the other students can see that you are taking it seriously; it shows the other students that there are consequences for uncooperative behaviour in your classroom; you are handling the situation in a non-confrontational manner.

Asking the student to write down his/her reasons for finding your lessons boring means that you avoid having to deal with a stroppy student's emotional response to the content of your lessons. This type of conversation will not be constructive for anyone involved. It may end up denting your confidence whilst making the student feel better that you have been 'told', especially if the student has been able to do it in front of their classmates. By asking student A to write down his/her points you are indicating that student A has to take responsibility for his/her behaviour while at the same time giving it importance by putting their points in the written form.

You can then control the content, the timing of the conversation and possibly also who attends the conversation. You may be able to suggest to the student that you wish another member of staff to be present in order that the student feels that their points are taken seriously. This gives you support if needed but it also gives the student the opportunity to back down as the student may decide at this stage that their reasons for finding your lessons 'boring' are more to do with them than you.

Instead, you may think it is appropriate to respond in writing to student A's points which can be given to them at the start of the next lesson. Again, this is a dialogue about learning which is in a format that a bright student might appreciate, but you should ensure that your Head of Department knows about this and is copied in to any letter that you write. Telling student A that you will respond to their concerns in a written form by next lesson can also help to defuse the immediate situation and ensure their cooperation for the rest of the lesson.

However, if you decide to take any of the above actions, you must make it absolutely clear that this is a 'one time offer'. You are happy to respond to student A's concerns in a conversation or in a letter but only this once. You cannot create a culture in your classroom of student A making emotive comments about your lessons on a regular basis which you then follow up all the time.

EXTRA NOTE

Bright but disruptive students can be damaging to the learning environment in your classroom so giving them the opportunity to write down their points can help 'clear the air' between you. It is then for you to decide if you think the student's points are valid and how you are going to react to them. You might wish to consult your Head of Department if you think some of the points are out of your control, e.g. lack of access to computers. You may decide to tell the class some of student A's points and how you are going to make improvements if you think it is appropriate.

It is a feature of successful teaching to receive feedback from students and using the written form to do this tends to ensure that the quality of the feedback you receive is more constructive and you can also control your reaction to the points that are made. If you feel it is appropriate, you might wish to extend the way you have handled student A's comments to the whole class. Towards the end of a lesson (a different one from the above lesson), ask all the students to give you some written feedback in the form of 'two positive points and two areas to improve' about your lessons. You can make this feedback as general or as specific as you wish – for example, students to give you comments about the teaching of a particular unit or types of teaching and learning activities.

However, in all cases, you must be seen to do something with the students' points. Sometimes, winning round a difficult class can be done by asking students for feedback and then being seen to react to it. For example, students may want more group work in lessons. Make sure that if you include group work in future lessons, you refer back to the feedback from the students and indicate that you are doing it because of what the students said. Some of the points that are made by the students may be impossible for you to implement – be honest about this and explain why you cannot do it. If needed, ask your Head of Department or another senior member of staff to come in and explain why an issue is school policy and not something that you can change.

Once you have built up a culture of constructive feedback in your classroom then a verbal discussion can also be incredibly helpful for you and the students. However, it may be some time before you feel able to do this as you do not want the conversation to turn into a 'free for all' about what is wrong with your lessons, the school, other teachers etc. You may find that promoting written feedback gives the students a framework to work within that can be expanded to a verbal discussion at an appropriate time.

A student asks to go to the toilet regularly

A student puts his/her hand up while you are talking to the rest of the class and in the teaching phase of your lesson and asks to go to the toilet after about ten minutes of the lesson. This is not the first time in one of your lessons that this student has done this and you are beginning to spot a regular pattern of this student asking to leave your lessons to go the toilet.

HOW DO YOU HANDLE THIS SITUATION?

1 You can say in front of the whole class '[Name of student] really so soon? Did you really forget to go to the toilet before you came to my lesson? No, you cannot go.'

The rest of the students might laugh at your comment but also the student is then likely to ensure that the focus of attention stays on them by saying 'Sir/Miss, I really do need to go. It's urgent – if you know what I mean. When you gotta go, you gotta go.' Are you still going to say 'no' at this point? If you do, is there a risk that the student might continue to disrupt your teaching by moving around on their chair and saying phrases like 'Come on Miss/Sir' etc.? At this point, the student has achieved their desired outcome which was clearly to disrupt your lesson, especially if you think that they timed their initial request to be the most disruptive.

Is there a risk that other students might join in the 'fun' and start saying 'Miss/Sir, you've got to let him/her go. What happens if there is an accident? You don't want that to happen, do you?' The momentum and focus of the lesson is now not only on you but also this student. At some point, you are going to have to do something about it and usually it will be to allow the student to leave to go to the toilet. What does this show about your authority in the classroom? Does it show that if you say 'no' but the students persist that you will always say 'yes'? Is the student likely to leave quietly when you do let them go and are they going to come back in again in a measured and calm manner? If the student has done this for maximum attention, are they likely to leave the room for a short time or just long enough to irritate you and make the point that this whole situation has been conducted at their pace? What are you going to say when this student returns? The other students are now involved and will be watching your reaction carefully. This has now escalated the situation to something that can undermine your authority in front of the students and therefore create a pattern that you may see emerge in future lessons.

2 You can say to the student '[Name of student] if you still need to go in five minutes, then you can ask me again.' This has given a solution to the problem and indicated to the student that you are not dealing with the request immediately. You are also suggesting that you do not consider this to be a genuine request which is why they need to ask again for you to take it seriously. This should give you enough time to finish the teaching phase of this part of your lesson and then talk to the student. Talking to the student might be easier than waiting for them to put up their hand again at another disruptive moment and ask the same question. If you let the student go to the toilet at this point of the lesson, you may wish to read (3) and think about whether talking to the student in the corridor on their return will also help to prevent this become a recurring issue.

3 As soon as you see the student put their hand up, you can indicate with a hand gesture that you wish for them to put their hand down. You can then go and stand near the student and finish what you are saying to the rest of the class. If the student is still trying to attract your attention while you are standing near to them then you can quickly say '[Name of student] I will finish talking in about three minutes and we can talk about whatever it is then.' Then move away and complete what you are saying as quickly as you can and organise the class with a quick discussion activity etc. Walk over to the student and ask what the problem is in a quiet and measured tone. The

student will then ask to go to the toilet and you will have to decide whether you want them to go or not. It may be easier to allow them to go at this point but give them a very strict time limit or they will make up the time at the end of the lesson. The student has not achieved their aim, which was to become the focus of your lesson, and you have dealt with the issue while not disrupting the others.

A further step you could take is, to catch the student just as he/she is about to enter your classroom again and ask them to have a quick word with you in the corridor. At this point, you could suggest that in the future, you wish for them to make any request to leave your classroom at an appropriate moment in the lesson for you and not for them. You could also suggest that you might mention this issue to their form tutor as you are concerned that the toilet breaks might be affecting their learning. This is making the point to the student that you are aware that there is a pattern emerging and also that you are prepared to take it further if needed.

Ask the student to return to the lesson and as the lesson develops, praise them at some point for their positive behaviour or contribution to your lesson. This will demonstrate to this student and the rest of the class that you value this student's positive behaviour.

EXTRA NOTE

Not letting students go to the toilet can be a problem, especially for younger students. If in doubt, it is always advisable to let the student go to the toilet but in a very strict time limit. A student who genuinely needed to go to the toilet will always get back in your time limit. A student who is using it as an excuse to get out of your lesson and perhaps be disruptive elsewhere will not usually return in your time limit. In all cases, you should record the time and number of minutes the student is out of your classroom.

If the student does return late to your lesson, you should ask them to wait outside and talk to them in the corridor. Make no accusations about what they might have been doing – just comment on the fact that they did not return in the allocated time. Tell them you have made a record of that and that as long as their contribution to the rest of the lesson is positive then you will not take it any further.

However, you may feel it is appropriate to mention the incidents to the student's form tutor or Head of Year to find out whether this is a recurring problem elsewhere and whether there are signs of vandalism etc. taking place during the times you recorded.

A student does not have the right equipment

A student does not have the right equipment for your lesson and this is not the first time. They always ask for it at the start of the lesson and don't attempt any work until they have it.

HOW DO YOU HANDLE THIS SITUATION?

1 Tell the student to go to the box where you have spare equipment and help themselves. Point out that it is marked as it is your stuff so they should not take it out of the classroom but put it back at the end of the lesson.

The student is now able to contribute to the lesson in a positive manner and there should be no reason for any disruptive behaviour. Undoubtedly, students should be encouraged to be prepared for their lessons and school, as being organised is definitely a life skill. However, this can be difficult for some students to manage just as it is not easy for some adults to be organised for events or situations that they encounter in life.

By giving the student the correct equipment you have also ensured there is no conflict between the two of you at the beginning of the lesson. Students who don't bring equipment to your lesson will also not be prepared for other lessons. They are likely to enjoy and engage with your lesson in a positive manner if you are not the third teacher that day who has told them off for not bringing the right equipment.

2 You can say '[Name of student] you never have the right equipment for my lesson. I am always lending you stuff. Why can't you remember to bring the right material? You will have to share with [name of another student] and remember to bring it next lesson otherwise I will put you in detention [or whatever is appropriate for your school context].'

This will deal with the issue as the student will have access to some equipment they can share. However, is this going to be a workable situation? Do the students need the equipment for a period of time, e.g. using a calculator to answer a range of questions? Do you know why this student keeps forgetting the equipment? Have you found out? Have you talked to anyone else about this student? Form tutor? Other subject staff? Is this student likely to disrupt others around them if they don't have access to the equipment when they need it? How are you going to maintain their focus on the task if they don't have the right equipment?

By the end of this conversation, have you really done anything to help them remember the equipment other than threaten them with a detention? Do you think this will have the required effect? What are you going to do when it happens next time?

3 Walk towards the student and say '[Name of student] you promised me that you would remember. Why can't you remember these things? Do I need to ring home about this? Is there a problem about you bringing in the right material? I suggest you leave the classroom since you clearly can't be part of this stage of the lesson and we will talk about it out there.'

How is the student going to react at this point? Is there any chance that they are embarrassed about not having the right equipment? Could there be a genuine reason for them not having the right material? The rest of the class are also now aware of the problem. Is the student more or less likely to cooperate with you and the activities for the rest of the lesson after the way you have spoken to them in the class? How are you going to resolve the issue when you talk to the student outside? How are you going to make them part of the lesson? If they are not bringing in the right equipment in order to avoid working in your lesson, sending them out is not going to solve this problem.

EXTRA NOTE

In more practical subjects, it is essential that students bring the right materials for the lesson in order to be part of the learning. However, if a student consistently does not seem able to remember to bring the right materials it would be advisable to see if you can find out the reasons for this. Talking to the form tutor or another teacher may help you find out the real reason and then with guidance from other staff, you can handle it in an appropriate context for your school.

SCENARIO 4

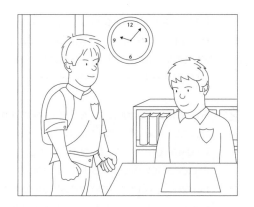

Students are late for your lesson

You have started your lesson and a group of students are late for your lesson. They do not enter quietly and are not very apologetic.

HOW DO YOU HANDLE THIS SITUATION?

1 Stop what you are doing and challenge the student/s for their lateness. Ensure that they apologise for being late and that they have a valid reason. If you are not happy with their reason or their attitude, tell them to wait outside the room. Don't take any excuses at this point; they have had their chance to be polite. Just move to the door, open it, indicate that they should leave and say that you will talk to them in a minute. Who is in control of the lesson at this point? Who is everyone looking at now? Is this the right type of message to be giving out to other students in the room? By sending out certain students are you reinforcing the message about the type of behaviour and attitude that is acceptable in your room?

Having sent the student/s out, you need to very quickly let them in again as they have the option of messing up your lesson with their delayed entrance or you having to spend extra time with them to bring them up to speed. After just a couple of minutes, open the door and let them in again and tell them where to sit and that you will talk to them in a minute. It doesn't matter how brief this exchange is as you have made the point by controlling their entrance into your room. Do make sure that you do talk to them during the lesson about what your expectations are of the right behaviour and attitude when they enter your classroom.

2   Allow the students to enter and mumble something to you and take their places. You choose to do this as you have started the lesson and you want to carry on for the benefit of those students who were on time to your lesson. However, what message does it indicate to students about who has control in your room? What does it indicate to them about the value that you place on your teaching and their learning? You may wish to talk to the students at an appropriate moment in the lesson about their reasons for being late and also indicate to them what will happen if they are late again. You may wish to refer to (1) for further guidance about what strategies you will tell them you will use in future.

3   Shut the door at the time that you consider it to be late for your lesson. For example, ensure that your door is shut if you think that after three minutes is late for your lesson. What will the students have to do in order to enter your room now? Will they have to knock? Will they be able to sneak in? Are you able to control more easily whether they enter or not? If appropriate, teach from the area of the classroom near the door so that you can easily control the students' entrance into the classroom if you realise that there is a group of students missing.

EXTRA NOTE

Telling students that they will make up the missed time at the end of the lesson does not really seem to work. You end up making them late for other lessons or taking up your break/lunchtime for something that could be dealt with in the lesson. However, if the lateness persists then creating a specific detention or letter home etc. seems to be more effective then 'tacking' a reprimand on the end of the lesson.

If a group of students are regularly late for a specific lesson you need to find out why. You need to find out from the students which lesson they have had previously and see if you can talk to this subject teacher about it. Are the students being let out late or are they making themselves late? It is always worth investigating further, especially if you see a pattern emerging.

SCENARIO 5

A student gives you a letter asking to be excused

A student (A) in a class that you have only recently started teaching has given you a letter which is meant to be written from his/her parent asking that they be excused from your lesson to go to a dentist appointment (or something similar). As you read it you become aware that it does not seem genuine. The wording is a little odd and the signature is unrecognisable as it is impossible to see any clues to the name of the parent from it. The student has given this to you at the beginning of the lesson and is insisting that they to leave in a minute.

WHAT DO YOU DO?

1 Tell the student that you need to check the letter out. How is the student going to react at this point? The student will probably say something along the lines that the letter is real and that it was written by their parent and are you suggesting that they are lying? The student could then say that they don't care what you say and they are going whether you like it or not. What are the other students doing at this point? If they are all entering the room at this point, will it have been done in an orderly manner? Are they all going to be listening to this conversation? If student A talks to you like this in front of the class, does this set the appropriate tone for the rest of the lesson? If this is a class that is still unfamiliar to you then they will probably take advantage of this situation by becoming talkative etc.

You need to ask student A to sit down in their seat and say you will talk to them about it within five minutes. If you are not specific about the time then they could start saying that they have to go and you will make them late etc. Insist that they sit down for five minutes while you deal with the rest of the class. Settle the rest of the class down and follow your usual class routines but make sure that the students are working in pairs on a verbal task etc. within five minutes.

Ask student A to come out of the classroom with you and explain how you do not like their attitude and behaviour. Do not talk to them in detail about it at this point as it is likely to cause more confrontation but use their previous behaviour as an excuse for having the letter checked out further. How you do this will depend on your school context and you will need to read (2) for ideas about how to do this. It is essential that you return to your class as quickly as possible with or without student A depending on the decision that you have made.

If you do end up agreeing to send Student A out of school with the letter as they are adamant that it is genuine then you need to follow it up as soon as possible. During the lesson (if appropriate) you should send an email/make a phone call to an appropriate member of staff to check out the situation. You could also send a responsible member of the class to Reception/School Office during the lesson with a note to check that student A signed out and that the letter was genuine. If you have concerns about this letter it is important that you do take some immediate action as you are responsible for the well-being and care of student A while they are in your class. Other people in the school need to be alerted to the fact that student A is not with you.

2   Thank student A for giving you the letter and ask him/her what time they think they need to leave. Move away from the student and tell the student firmly to sit down and do not continue with the conversation. As soon as you can – even as students are arriving – ask a responsible member of the class to take the letter to the school Office/Reception etc. and write a short note on the top of the letter which says 'Can you check this out asap please?' Start the lesson in your usual orderly manner and if need be, indicate to student A that you will talk to them shortly. Hopefully, two things will happen in a short period of time. The student will return with a note that says 'Yes, this is fine' or student A will be asked to go to Reception. Either way you have dealt with the situation in a non-confrontational manner and it has been taken out of your hands.

However, you can send student A to Reception/School Office and miss out the responsible student, especially if the school policy is that a student needs to sign out to leave the school premises, but somehow you need to check that (a) the student goes to Reception/School Office and (b) you are not condoning truancy by not checking the details of the letter if you think it is not genuine.

This situation can be avoided for class teachers if the school policy is that form tutors/pastoral staff sign the letter at the beginning of the day if the letter is handed in then. However, inevitably some students will not do this especially if they are attempting to truant. If you do end up sending student A to Reception with the letter and they do not return to your lesson then you need to follow it up as soon as possible. A quick email/phone call to Reception/School Office to check that student A did sign out and that the letter was fine would be advisable.

3   You can tell the student that they not allowed to go and that they will stay in your classroom until further information is received. You can tell them that if the parent is really coming to collect the student then Reception/School Office will let you know when they have arrived and student A can go then. Student A is likely to tell you that they are meeting the parent at the dentist/doctor etc. and that they are not coming to school. However, you do not want to get into the details by asking questions such as 'How are you going to get there?' as this will just add fuel to the confrontation. Student A is not likely to react very well to the fact that you have not allowed them to leave so be prepared for a negative reaction and behaviour for the rest of your lesson. You need to end the conversation as quickly as possible, move away from student A and focus on the rest of the class.

If student A is becoming very disruptive then you might want to send a responsible student (or email/ring) to Reception/School Office/form tutor to check out the details. Telling student A that you are doing this might calm them down but it could make them say 'Well I will go to Reception myself and I will sort it out there as you can't make me stay here.' At this point, you should let student A leave the classroom and not stop them. Keep calm and tell the rest of the class to keep working while you just let someone know that student A has left your class. Don't try and pretend it hasn't happened or chase after student A shouting at them. The student will not come back at this point and leaving your class will only create further tension with the remaining students.

The action you take next will depend on the context of your school. You need to tell someone more senior that student A is no longer in your classroom and could be heading off site without permission. You are responsible for the well-being and welfare of student A and someone else needs to know that they are no longer with you. This can be done via email/phone call/sending a note/going to your Head of Department/School Office – you should try and do one of these during your lesson rather than wait till the end.

If needed, set your class on a verbal discussion task or something similar that will give you the five minutes you need to take this action. Ideally, you should not leave your classroom and send a student with a note (send email etc.) but if that is not possible you need to go and tell an appropriate member of staff. If necessary, ask another member of staff in the classroom next to you to send a student from their class with a note or contact the right person on your behalf. Do not worry about doing this as it is important that you feel you have taken the appropriate action.

Before the next lesson with student A you need to have a discussion with them about their behaviour. You should try and do this with the student's form tutor/Head of Year or your Head of Department. You need to explain to the student about how badly they handled the situation and how a similar situation should be handled in the future. It doesn't matter whether the letter proves to be genuine or not – it is the way that student A behaved that needs to be discussed. The student needs to understand that there are consequences to leaving your lesson without permission.

EXTRA NOTE

The action you are able to take does depend on the context of your school and the small amount of knowledge that you have about the individual student. Experience tends to tell you whether a student has a genuine letter or not, but do not be intimidated into making a decision you feel is wrong. It is perfectly acceptable to check out the details of the letter with the School Office/Reception/form tutor if you can do it in a manner which is not disruptive for the rest of the students. The increasing use of emails as a means of communication in schools can help you with this matter but sometimes the good old-fashioned approach of sending a student with a note can achieve more immediate results. Do not worry about involving other members of staff (in the next classroom) in this matter, especially if you have a difficult class and do not feel that you can leave them. The other member of staff can give you some quick advice or take the matter out of your hands. The remaining students in the classroom and other staff involved need to see that you have taken firm and quick action for them to feel that the situation has been handled appropriately.

A student is leaning out of the window

You have entered the classroom at the start of the lesson and found that a student is leaning out of the window. You have asked them to move away from the window but they have ignored your first request.

WHAT DO YOU DO?

1 You can stay where you are and shout their name and threaten some kind of sanction if they don't move away from the window. However, what happens if they ignore you as they 'can't hear you'? What will the rest of the class be doing at this point? Is there a risk that some of the other students will join in and lean out of the window too?

2 You can walk over to the window and talk firmly to the student while gently pulling them away from the window if you think that is appropriate. You are allowed to use appropriate physical restraint if it is necessary to stop a student from injuring him or herself or someone else or damaging property. If you think the student is in danger of falling out of the window then you will have to judge the situation and decide whether physical contact is appropriate. How is the student going to react to you doing this? What happens if they pull away from you? Are you likely to fall over? Could the student say 'Don't touch me. Get off me.' You may then end up dealing with an angry student who is speaking to you in an inappropriate manner which will then escalate the situation even further. What has happened to the atmosphere at the start of your lesson? What are the other students going to be doing at this point?

3 You can walk quickly over to the window and stand close to the student and speak very sharply '[Name of student] move away from the window now.' Is the student more likely to listen now that you are standing close to them? The other students are less likely to become involved as your physical presence in that area of the classroom will deter them. Repeat the directive again in a firm manner. The student will hopefully comply with your demand and if they do not then you will need to add in sanctions. You then need to quickly start your lesson in an orderly manner as the behaviour of this student can be a catalyst for other poor behaviour if you give the students an opportunity. Additionally, you need to talk to the student at a later point in the lesson and explain the reasons why his/her actions were inappropriate. During this conversation you need to be very specific about sanctions that will take place if they do the same thing again.

Try to avoid having this conversation immediately after the incident as it will take up time, the student is likely to be confrontational as their classmates will be the audience and you are delaying the start of the lesson and giving opportunities for other students to engage in disruptive behaviour.

EXTRA NOTE

In order to avoid a similar situation, you might want to consider why the student was hanging out of the window. Were you late for the lesson? Are the students allowed in the room before you – is this something that you could change? Is there usually a pacey start to your lesson? Do the students know that there is some 'hanging about' time before the learning starts? Is this something that you could change?

A student is listening to music in your lesson

A student is wearing earphones and listening to music while they are meant to be working or while you are teaching.

WHAT DO YOU DO?

1 Stop what you are doing and say '[Name of student] – stop listening to your music and start working.' The risk of this approach is that the student will think it is funny to pretend that they have not heard you since they are 'listening' to music. Are the other students going to laugh at you or the student? How are you going to make sure that they do take their earphones out?

Could the student react negatively to this approach and say something along the lines of 'I wasn't listening to music. Why do you always pick on me? [Name of another student] has their earphones in but you don't tell them off, do you?'

Try not to respond to their negative behaviour and comments and state that you would like them to remove their earphones as wearing earphones usually gives the impression that someone is listening to music. Then smile and walk away to avoid any further confrontation.

2 Move towards the student and mime that they should remove the earphones. You can usually do this without stopping what you are saying and it causes the minimum amount of disruption to the other students while making it quite clear what you want the student to do. If they don't comply then you may find standing next to them and asking them quietly to remove their earphones will then work.

You may feel that it is advisable to talk to the student at a later stage in the lesson about why they didn't respond immediately to your request to remove the earphones. It is important to address all the smaller issues of behaviour management from students in your lesson as ultimately this will help to deter bigger behaviour management problems in the future.

3 Move right next to the student and ask them why they think it is appropriate to wear earphones and listen to music in your lesson. This approach is dependent on when you decide to do this in the lesson. Sometimes, students still have their earphones in but music is not being played, which is why they can get defensive if you tell them to stop listening to music. On some occasions, it can be beneficial to ask students to justify their behaviour, in this case, listening to music in your lesson. They clearly know that it is not appropriate behaviour but they have made an active choice to do it. A discussion about the reasons for the chosen course of behaviour can have a longer impact on some students than simply telling them not to do something.

A student is throwing small items across the room to other students

Students are meant to be completing their own work and you have been helping other students in the class. However, you become aware that a student is throwing small items across the room to other students – bits of rubber, small pieces of paper, bits of pen etc. The student is trying to do it without you seeing them but other students are complaining about what is happening.

WHAT DO YOU DO?

1 Stop what you are doing and say '[Name of student] – please stop throwing things at [names of other students]. It is not something that we do in this lesson and it is disruptive to other students plus you will have to stay behind and clear up the mess.'

What is the student likely to say at this point? 'It wasn't me, why do you think it was me? You always think it is me. It is not fair, you always pick on me. You don't tell off [name of other student], he/she does it too but you don't see that.'

How are you going to react to this? Who is everyone looking at? What does it indicate about the relationship that you have with this student? What does it also indicate about how they feel they can talk to you? What have you indicated by using the word 'please'?

At this point, you may wish to move closer to the student and crouch down to their level to discuss it further. This allows the rest of the class to focus on their work but it also shows them that you are dealing with it. During the conversation with the student, you will need to be very clear about your reasons for stating in front of the class that the student *had* thrown items, as this will help to defuse their feeling that they are 'picked on'. You may wish to read (3) about the possible content of this conversation.

2   Give the student a warning by commenting on their behaviour '[Name of student] – you are clearly throwing bits of pen at [name of other student] and this is your first warning. If I see you do it again, I will ask you to move to [specify a place in the room] or you will stay behind at the end of the lesson' etc. After you have delivered this warning I suggest that you move round the room and stand near the student that you suspect. You also need to engage positively with this student as quickly as possible after this warning. You need to give them a small five-minute achievable target or comment positively on work that they have already done etc. If you do set a five-minute target, make sure you return and see that it has been achieved then set another one. Each time using praise.

Have you given a choice to this student? Are they clear about the consequences of their actions? Do you think your positive attention will have an impact on this student? What are the reasons for the student throwing items in the first place? Are they bored? Trying to irritate you? Drawing attention to themselves? Will your positive actions offset their negative behaviour?

3   Move from where you are standing in the classroom to the desk where this particular student is sitting. Then at an appropriate moment, try and see the room from their angle, maybe sit down next to them and help them. See if you can see evidence of the thrown items around other students. If you can see evidence of items or are confident about their actions, talk to the student about it.

You may wish to start by saying, 'Why can I see bits of pen around [name of student]? Do you think someone has thrown it?' Wait for their response. 'Do you think you could have thrown them? From this angle, it looks like you could have thrown those items.' Wait for their response. 'Where are you getting the bits from? Why are you throwing them? Are there any other students involved in this?' Wait for their response. You need to make clear that if you see items being thrown again by anyone in the class (don't specifically mention the name of the student) then certain consequences will take place. You will tell them to move, stay behind after class, put them in detention etc. – whatever is appropriate for your school context.

Before you get up and move away, comment on the positive behaviour of the student during that conversation and make it clear that you will be disappointed if their positive behaviour doesn't continue. You may find giving them a small target will help too. For example, write four lines in the next five minutes, complete an activity in the textbook etc. However, you need to check on this student within the time limit to see whether they have completed this target otherwise there will be no benefit to them in continuing with their positive behaviour as you are not going to be able to reward it with a positive comment.

How do you think the student will behave during that one-to-one conversation? Have you given them the option to 'put their case forward'? Have you also spelt out very clearly what will happen if they choose to take the wrong action? Despite a negative act, have you managed to end the conversation on a positive note? Have you also given them a signal about how to behave positively in the lesson, e.g. set them an achievable target?

A student refuses to work with a teaching assistant

You have introduced your lesson and the learning outcomes etc. You have asked the students to work independently on an activity. It is at this point that you notice that a student who regularly works with a teaching assistant has moved and is not sitting with the teaching assistant any more. The teaching assistant is now sitting alone and asking you to come over and talk to them.

HOW DO YOU HANDLE THIS SITUATION?

1 While still standing in your position in the classroom say loudly '[Name of student] why have you moved? I have not given you permission to move – move back now. Thanks.' Break eye contact with the student and work with another student while monitoring whether student A has followed your instructions. At this point, you may also wish to ask the TA to work with other students and be very specific about the outcomes that you wish to see from these students after they have received the TA's support. This will indicate the value that you put on the TA's work with students.

If student A has not moved by now, then you need to walk over to them and find out why they have not moved. Student A is likely to escalate the situation by telling you that they don't want to move back, they don't want to work with the TA as they think it is rubbish that they always have to work with a TA. They might even ask you why they need to work with a TA etc. At this point, the other students will probably start listening to the conversation plus you also have to remember that you have the TA sitting in the classroom too. In order to calm the situation down, you might need to ask student A to leave the class at this point. However, the student is not likely to do this quietly or calmly and will ensure that further disruption is made to your lesson. Leave the student outside for a few minutes and ensure that your class and the TA are working successfully.

You can then go outside and talk to the student about their behaviour. You may wish to read (3) at this point and see how this discussion and follow-up action should be conducted. However, if you think that student A's behaviour has been too inappropriate then it might not be advisable to let them return to the lesson as (3) suggests. Instead, you might need to take action that is appropriate for your school context which means that the student does not return for the rest of this particular lesson. However, if you decide to remove the student from your lesson then, as stated in (3), it is essential that you and another member of staff talk to student A before they come to another one of your lessons. If student A does not return to your lesson, you must be very clear in your support of your TA and be seen to be working together for the rest of your lesson. You should also discuss future action about student A with your TA at the end of your lesson.

2   From your position in the classroom say, '[Name of student] why have you moved? I did not give you permission to move.' As you say this, move closer to student A and indicate to them that you wish for them to move back to their original position. You could also ask the TA to explain why they think student A has moved. This gives support to the TA as you are clearly consulting them and you can discuss together how inappropriate student A's behaviour has been. Student A is not likely to move back at this point as they will feel embarrassed to do so.

Therefore, you could suggest that student A moves back for ten minutes while the TA ensures that they have understood the task and say that you will ask the TA to work with other students during the lesson. However, you should make this suggestion by including the TA in this conversation. Move right next to the student's desk and quietly repeat the suggestion and give them a choice. If they do not move and work with the TA for the next ten minutes then you will put them in a school detention (or whatever is appropriate for your school context). Try to avoid giving the student the choice of leaving the classroom for ten minutes as they may take the option to leave since you have strongly indicated how much you want them to work with the TA and they clearly want to defy you.

Hopefully, the student will move and work with the TA for next the ten minutes. Meanwhile, ask the TA to work with other specific students as this will help them to leave student A if they are still being uncooperative which will avoid another confrontational situation. Monitor what is happening and ensure that the TA does not spend more than ten minutes with student A. Try to ensure that the TA is busy with other students for most of the lesson, and for the rest of the lesson that you both help/monitor student A's progress. Towards the end of the lesson, praise student A (if appropriate) for their work and state that they made the right choice as the student has been able to stay in the lesson and has achieved 'x' and 'y'.

As the rest of the students are leaving, ask student A to stay briefly and talk to them (ensure that the classroom door is open). Ask them if there is going to be a repeat of their behaviour in future lessons. Ask if they preferred the TA working with them for short periods of time. If the student handles this conversation appropriately then say that you and the TA will implement some changes but do remind the student that moving and refusing to work with the TA was not the best way of handling the situation.

You also need to talk to the TA at the end of that lesson or at another point (definitely before the next lesson) and ask the TA what action they would like to have happen. Make the suggestion about working for short periods with student A and working with other students too. If you are both happy with this, implement these changes and see what happens in future lessons.

You may still feel you should let another appropriate member of staff know about the incident but also how you have solved it (Special Needs Co-ordinator/form tutor/Head of Year) etc. in case student A is doing this in other classes or it is a result of other issues that you are have not been made aware of.

3 Walk over to the TA, check that no bad behaviour has been shown towards them and ask if they can think of any reasons for student A's behaviour. Ask the TA to go and work with another student (student B) and explain what you wish them to do. You should ask the TA to work with a range of other students during the course of the lesson too. Explain to student B that they will have a teaching assistant working with them today for this activity and explain how you think the TA can help them.

You then need to talk to student A and this is probably best done outside the classroom as the student has already clearly indicated that they are not in a cooperative mood by refusing to work with the TA.

The meeting outside the classroom should be short and is not meant to uncover many of the reasons why this student is refusing to work with the TA. You just need to resolve the issue for this lesson and then follow it up later on when you have more time. Ask the student to explain what caused them to behave in this way. The student's answer will probably range from being angry with the TA for something that was said/done in a previous lesson to a shrug of the shoulders followed by 'Don't know'. Whatever the response may be, explain to student A that the way they handled the situation was inappropriate and outline to them the other ways they could have acted:

- talk to you before the beginning of the lesson
- talk to their Head of Year if there was a problem about a specific issue
- talk to their form tutor etc.

Explain that you will refer the incident to the Head of Year/Special Needs Co-ordinator/form tutor as there is clearly an issue that needs to be resolved. However, for this lesson tell the student that they should return to their original seat and start working without their TA. Take the student back into the classroom and escort them back to their original seat. Explain briefly the work that you wish the student to complete. You might need to abbreviate some of the task so that they stand a chance of completing some of it in the allocated time. During the rest of the lesson, set the student short, timed activities in order to help them complete the longer tasks that you might be setting the rest of the class. Continuous monitoring of the student's work throughout the lesson will give you the opportunity to praise the student but it will also mean that the student has little opportunity to engage in low-level, off-task behaviour which could be disruptive to your lesson.

However, you also need to support the TA and ensure that their status is maintained with the other students in the lesson. Attempt to spend some time talking to the TA during the lesson and also asking them to work with different students in the room who might not usually receive support. Be seen to be asking the TA for feedback about the progress of specific students in the class so that the students are clearly aware of how you value the TA's input to your lesson.

As the lesson draws to a close, praise the student (if appropriate) for what they have achieved in your lesson. Remind them that you will refer the incident of not working with their TA to other senior staff as this is clearly an issue that needs to be resolved for everyone.

At the end of the lesson, after the students have left, ensure that you talk to the TA and find out how they felt about the lesson. (If you can't do this immediately at the end of the lesson, make sure that you fix a time to meet the TA during the day, break or lunchtime etc.) Ask them to tell you what action they think should be taken about student A's behaviour. Has this happened before in other lessons with this student? What do they think the problem was?

You need to refer this incident to an appropriate member of staff explaining what happened in the lesson, what you did about it, how you have talked to the TA and how you both think that certain action should take place before the next lesson. It is important that the appropriate member of staff has spoken to student A before your next lesson as this incident cannot be repeated. Student A's behaviour may be due to factors that are outside of your classroom and therefore your control which is why you cannot be expected to deal with this type of incident on a regular basis.

Giving out a seating plan to students as they enter your classroom

You are putting the students into a new seating plan – it doesn't really matter whether this is a class you know or not. It is the way you handle it at the start of the lesson that can set the tone for the rest of the lesson.

WHICH WAY IS LIKELY TO CAUSE YOU THE LEAST PROBLEMS?

1 Students enter the classroom and you have put the seating plan on the board at the front of the class. You are standing near your desk and say as they walk in 'Morning everyone, we are going to have a new seating plan today. Can you sit where it tells you to please.'

What do you do if students come up to you and start saying 'I am not sitting there. I hate [name of other student]. It is not fair, you always make me sit with people I don't like. Why do we have to have a seating plan anyway?'

You will probably end up with a crowd of students around your desk. How are you going to disperse them without being confrontational? What does the word 'please' signify about the seating plan? Are you suggesting that it is something you are inviting them to do or simply expecting them to do?

2   You stand by the door with the seating plan in your hand and only let students in when you tell them where to sit. What happens when students start to say 'I am not sitting there. Why do I always have to sit with [name of student]. These seating plans are stupid and I am not sitting there.'

You are at the door and still trying to get everyone in the classroom. What are the students, who are not sitting where they need to, being allowed to do? How are you going to sort this out? What happens if students have sat in the wrong place on purpose while you are still informing other students of their places? How are you going to deal with the students who have sat in the wrong places?

Try to get the rest of the students inside the classroom before dealing with those who are sitting in the wrong place, otherwise you stand the chance of the remaining students sitting in the wrong place just to wind you up. Ask all the students to stand up and then, by standing near the students who need to move, sort out the seating plan.

If you have the seating plan on the board so all the students can see it then it is easier to make sure the students move into the right places. However, standing near the students you want to move does help as your physical presence is more likely to ensure their cooperation. If some students are still resisting the new seating arrangements then you will need to give them a choice. See (3) for ideas of choices. It is important that students do comply with your seating plan as it is part of your bigger behaviour management strategy. By telling the student that the move to the new seat is for the rest of the lesson you are diffusing the current situation. This might not be the truth but is more likely to make the student move than by suggesting that it is a permanent move.

3   You stand by the door and greet everyone with 'Morning, we are going to have a new seating plan today and I have spent time making sure that everyone is going to be with a successful learning partner.' You then step away from the door and step back into the classroom facing the room.

You stand in a strong position in the classroom with the seating plan on the board behind you. You then make eye contact with all the students as they walk towards you and try to give them an individual greeting. You keep reminding them of the seating plan and asking them to sit in the right places. You also try to make some individual comments about why you think a specific student is going to work really well with another student which is why you have organised the seating plan in the way that you have.

As the negative comments start, you are in the right place in the room to deal with them in a non-confrontational manner by addressing the individuals immediately and directly. You simply tell them that they need to sit there for the initial part of the lesson (or give a specific time limit) and if there is a real problem, they can talk to you about it at some point in the lesson. You DO NOT let them move to where they wish to sit.

If they will not cooperate, give them the choice, 'You need to sit in that place for the first part of the lesson (give a specific time limit) and if there is a problem you can talk to me about it later or you will have to leave the classroom for a short time so that I can work with the students who clearly want to learn in my lesson today.'

You will have to select the moment when you allow the student to talk to you about the seating plan. You will have to ensure that the student does not do it when the whole class can watch the interaction between you. It should be done while the other students are engaged in an activity or you can delay it to the end of the lesson. Most students don't feel so strongly about their seating arrangement that they wish to spend time with you at the end of the lesson discussing it.

However, during any discussion about the seating plan, you need to repeat the reasons for creating the seating plan in the structure that you have. Making them believe that it is not permanent seems to help. Once they have cooperated with the seating plan in one lesson it is easier to ensure that they stick to it in future ones.

Making the students believe at the start of the lesson that they don't have to sit in the seating plan for the whole lesson can help defuse the situation in the short term. This might not be the truth but it allows you to start your lesson and put the focus on the important business of learning and teaching.

EXTRA NOTE

You may find that some of these issues are avoided if you create two seating plans – that you identify by colours, famous characters etc. You can have one seating plan when you state to the class that they have 'learning partners' and one where they have 'talk partners'. The 'talk partners' seating plan can be created more around friendship groups if you think this is appropriate. The 'learning partners' seating plan is organised to help students maximise their learning. It might be appropriate to seat the students boy-girl-boy-girl or by ability etc. Defining the seating plans in this way allows the students to understand the purpose of the seating plans and can cause less resentment. It also helps you to balance out the groupings depending on the content of the lesson and ensure more cooperation from the students. It also allows you to vary the pace and activities of the lesson as there is no reason why you cannot move from one seating plan to another during a lesson.

11

Students enter the classroom noisily

Students start to enter your classroom after break or lunchtime with a considerable amount of noise. Some students are coming over to tell you about why they haven't done their homework, don't have an exercise book etc. You are at your desk, putting the last few touches to the lesson.

HOW DO YOU HANDLE THIS TYPE OF SITUATION?

1 While you are at your desk, sorting out the last few things for the lesson, tell the class to settle down and not be so noisy but let them sit down in their places. You are confident that you will be able to demand silence when you are ready to start the lesson. Talk to the students who are telling you about their homework etc. as this will help solve problems further on in the lesson.

How long are you going to spend with these students standing round your desk? Can you see what the other students are doing? How are you going to get their attention at the start of the lesson? Do you have a signal that they recognise? What message does it send out about the ownership of the lesson and the room? Is there anything for the students to do as they sit down? Is there an expected routine for them to follow when they enter the classroom?

2   Walk to the door and send all the students out again as they are too noisy. Make them line up in silence and then stand by the door as they walk past you into their places.

What has this done to the atmosphere of the lesson? What happens if some students are slow to leave the classroom when you send them all out again? What happens if they are not silent in the corridor and start laughing instead? Are you going to be able to maintain their silence as they sit down; what are you going to be doing? Are you able to keep your eye on them all as you take the register or give out the resources for the lesson?

3   Put up your hand and indicate to the students that they stop entering the classroom. Position yourself just inside the classroom and greet the students as they walk past you with a positive or individual greeting. Don't react to comments by the students about homework or having to leave the lesson early etc. Just keep reminding the students to sit down and start the task that is on the board behind you. Walk over to individual students and remind them to take their pens out etc. and complete the task that is on the board in front of them. Only once you can see that all the students are behaving in a positive way do you move back to your desk and start to take the register and give out resources etc. Still, do not let students interrupt you with points about homework etc. Just tell them that you will hear about it later.

What message have you sent out to the students about who is in charge of the lesson? Have you indicated the importance of having a meaningful and purposeful start to the lesson? Have you also indicated to them that you are happy to see them but have not started the lesson in a confrontational manner?

EXTRA NOTE

If you follow the example in (3), as soon as the other students are working on the activities of the lesson ensure that you go and talk to the students who had concerns about their homework, lack of exercise book etc.

CHAPTER 2

MANAGING THE BEHAVIOUR OF STUDENTS DURING THE MAIN PHASE OF YOUR LESSON

What do you do when a student . . .

SCENARIO 1

A student calls you by your first name

You have started your lesson and students are working on paired/individual activities. One of the students puts up his/her hand and says '[Your first name] can you come and help me with this please?' The rest of the class laugh.

HOW DO YOU HANDLE THIS?

1 You can say to the student: 'If it was up to me then you could call me by my first name. However, it is school policy to address staff with surnames and I think you should follow the school rules, don't you?' This can help to defuse the situation and be seen to put the blame elsewhere.

However, another student is likely to then say 'Well Kate, if we don't tell anyone then can we call you by your first name in your lessons if you don't mind?' Students have a fascination with calling teachers by their first names as they are probably the only adults in their lives whose surnames they have to use on a regular basis. This then becomes a compelling situation that students wish to subvert or at least explore further. You will have to decide whether you think it is appropriate to allow students to call you by your first name but you should check it with your Head of Department first. You can tell the students that you are going to ask your Head of Department and you will get back to them. You need to think carefully about why you are going to allow your students to use your first name. What is your motive? Is it that you think it will make the students like you more? Is that important? Are they going to achieve more by calling you by your first name? Will it create a more conducive learning atmosphere in the classroom if they do this? Is that important?

If you do decide to allow it, the students in this class will inevitably tell other students that you teach and they will all insist that they call you by your first name. This may be fine with classes that are manageable but there will be other classes in the future that will test you. It is at this point that you may find the professional distance that using a surname gives you is needed; however, once you have agreed to not use your surname it will be impossible to reinstate it.

2 You can say 'What did you say [name of student? Did you call me by my first name – Kate? Do I know you out of school? Are we friends? Why do you think you can call me Kate?' Wait for some of the answers for these questions. By saying your name a few times out loud, it takes the taboo out of saying it in your classroom. If you simply refer to 'my first name' rather than actually saying your name, it will make it still seem something fun to say in your classroom.

Ask the student a couple of times to explain why they think they can call you by your first name. By doing this you are asking them to explain their behaviour rather than telling them off for it. If other students then call you by your first name during the lesson, ask them to explain why they think they can do this. Have you given them permission to do so? Do they call other teachers by their first name? Would they call their boss at work by their first name if they didn't say 'You can call me by my first name'? Would they call the head teacher by their first name? Why or why not? Asking the students questions like this will lead onto a discussion about status. Who has status in society and who does not? How do you acquire certain status?

Inevitably, students will say that you are allowed to call them by their first names so why can't they call you by your first name? You might want to talk about identity at this point. You might wish to say that you call them by their first names as this is what gives them identity to you and each other within the school. What would be the alternative? Master or Miss? Would that give a true indication of who they are as young people? As young people, their names are one of the ways of indicating their identity as they don't have much else to show this at this stage of their lives: no jobs, cars, houses, few qualifications etc. This is why it is important that in a school environment where they are meant to be learning as an individual, that teachers use their first name. Remind them that students prefer it when teachers know them as individuals as most students feel that personal knowledge about their learning preferences is what helps them learn.

Conversely, it is not important for students to know teachers on a personal basis in order for teachers to do their job properly. The use of surnames indicates the professional rather than the personal nature of the relationship between a student and a teacher, which is why it is important. Using the first name of a teacher indicates an intimacy that is not appropriate or needed for successful learning and teaching to take place. Teachers are professionals and the use of surnames indicates their status within a school environment just as surnames of doctors, judges, consultants etc. are used within their professional environment.

All the above points explain some of the reasons why schools insist that students use surnames when addressing teachers and you may have others that you think are appropriate. Explaining the reasons for the rules tends to help defuse the situation and help to avoid the students using your first name again. If using your first name happens again at least you can now point out to the student/s that you had talked about it with them and explained it and you thought that everyone understood the reasons. At this point, you can also throw in for good measure that it is school policy and if they really feel strongly about it then maybe they should take it up with the head teacher.

3   Say from the front of the class '[Name of student] you do not talk to a member of staff like that and leave the classroom now.' There is a possibility that the student might say 'Of course [your first name] I will leave now.' At this point, the rest of the class will be laughing and the attention is now firmly on this student and possibly others, if more students join in. The student will probably leave whilst still saying your first name in different contexts and then you will need to deal with the student outside and the rest of the students in the classroom. What are you going to say at this point? How are you going to stop the laughing? How are you going to stop other students from saying your first name or any other nickname that they might have for you during the rest of the lesson and for future ones?

A student falls asleep during your lesson

You are in the teaching phase of your lesson and you have noticed that a student has put their head on the desk and has not moved for a period of time while you have been teaching. You assume that he/she is asleep.

WHAT DO YOU DO?

1 From your position in the classroom, ask the student who is sitting next to the sleeping student to wake them up. This will inevitably make the rest of the class laugh as the student is likely to shout or make the sleeping student jump in some way. This will cause a few moments of amusement at the sleeping student's expense which will reinforce the fact that you do not like students falling asleep. However, it does not address the underlying issue as to how the sleeping student is likely to react when awoken in such a manner. Are they likely to engage in your lesson in a positive manner from this point forward? What have you also done to the atmosphere of your lesson? How are you going to ensure that all the students' attention is back on what they should be doing?

2 Shout the student's name quite loudly and say '[Name of student] are you listening? Didn't you go to bed early enough? I have just been talking about . . . could you tell me what the answer is to the question . . .'

Is the student likely to be able to answer your question? How are they going to react to you singling them out in this way? Are they likely to behave in a positive manner at this stage? Are the other students going to laugh at him/her? Are they likely to lift their head up, smile and then put their head down again as they cannot deal with the situation? What are you going to do now? Do you know why this student has fallen asleep? What are all the other students doing at this point? Are they focused on the learning or on you making fun of one of their classmates?

3 At an appropriate moment in the lesson when the other students are working, walk over to the student's desk and talk to them quietly. Ask them to wake up and sit up. Give them a few seconds to follow that instruction and ask them to talk to you in the corridor as you are concerned about their well-being. Don't make it a confrontational situation; if you keep your voice calm, the student is more likely to comply.

Once outside, ask the student why they are so tired. What is going on? Do they think it is appropriate to fall asleep in your lesson? You may wish to tell them that you are going to mention this episode to their form tutor/Head of Year etc. as you are concerned about how tired they are. However, by making the point that you are going to refer it on, you are also pointing out that you consider this sort of behaviour inappropriate although you have not done this in a confrontational manner. Additionally, you MUST make sure that you do let this student's form tutor know about what has happened as there may be some extra information that they can share with you. You could ask the form tutor to mention this incident to the student before your next lesson. This way, the student is aware that you have followed up on the incident as you are concerned but it also indicates that you considered it to be inappropriate behaviour.

Depending on how they handle this conversation, you might feel it is appropriate to suggest that they go and get themselves a drink of water and wash their face to help wake up. Then tell them to return to your lesson promptly.

By talking to the student outside of the classroom, you have defused the embarrassment factor for them but you have also indicated to the other students that it was an event that you took seriously.

EXTRA NOTE

You may also wish to think about the atmosphere of your classroom especially in lessons after lunchtime. Is your room too hot? Are any windows open? The temperature in a classroom can give a very clear indication of the type of behaviour that will be found in the room. When walking into someone else's classroom, the first thing that hits you is the temperature and the stuffiness of the room. Dozy looking students or evidence of poor behaviour tend to be a clear clue that the room is too hot for the number of people in it. Some kind of circulation of air is essential for allowing everyone's brains to work. Watching videos or films is always a typical time when windows are shut because the blinds/curtains are down but this really adds to the heat of the room and the lethargy of the students.

When windows are open, students often complain of the room feeling too cold as teenagers never seem to come dressed for the weather. Students can insist that it is too cold and they cannot work etc. However, a compromise can be to have the windows open and shut for timed periods of your lesson. This allows you to control the temperature while ensuring the cooperation of the students in your lesson.

A *student is copying the work of another student*

Students are sitting in pairs at desks but are meant to be working independently on a written activity in your lesson. However, on one table you can see that every time student A writes something down, student B looks down at student A's work and writes something down too. You can only assume that student B is copying the work of student A.

HOW DO YOU HANDLE THIS SITUATION?

1 Stand still and do not walk over to the students but ask immediately for student B to bring their work to you and the work of student A. You can then compare them and make it clear where you think the copying has taken place. You can then ask student B why they felt it was appropriate to copy and why they couldn't think of their own ideas. How cooperative is student B going to be at this point? Have you drawn the other students' attention to this? You may feel that this is an appropriate action as you wish the other students to realise that you do not approve of copying, but do not be surprised if student B does not respond very well to your comments. Is this method going to allow you to establish the reasons for student B copying? How are you going to ensure that this does not happen again? What has happened to your relationship with student B? Is he/she going to be more or less likely to ask you for help in the future if they do not understand, or are they going to continue to copy as a coping strategy?

2   You can walk round the classroom, stopping to read students' work and making positive or targeted comments about their writing. Move round to the table where student A and student B are sitting and watch the body language of student B. Does their body language change? Do they make it easy for you to read their work? You can reach down and pick up their work and read it a little more closely. You can then bend down to be at student B's level and ask them to discuss the work with you. Ask some questions about the meaning of what they have written. Ask them to justify the words/terminology/ideas that they have chosen but in a non-confrontational manner. You need to check whether they have understood what they are meant to be doing and if not, then clearly you will help them. Some students are very good at hiding their lack of understanding or feeling of incompetency by becoming very good at copying just enough of another student's work to make it look like their own work.

It is a common mistake to assume that seeing lots of 'heads down and writing' is a true indicator of learning and of the level of students' understanding. Some students can simply be copying down the key parts of their neighbour's writing so that it looks as if they understand the task.

However, if you are confident that student B does know what they doing after you have questioned them, stand up and say quietly, 'Well done [student B's name], you clearly understand what you are doing and I am really pleased by what you have done here and here [refer specifically to the work]. There is no reason, then, for you to to copy [student A's name] work is there?' Smile and then walk away.

Student B will feel supported by the intervention you have put in place but you have also made the point in a non-confrontational manner that you know what has been going on. Student B is likely to look a little embarrassed and then carry on with their own individual work. You have also managed to sort out this situation with very few of the other students being aware and have avoided a possible confrontation.

3   You can stand still and do not walk over to the students but say loudly '[Name of student B] I would like to see your work in five minutes to check that you are well on your way to completing the task. When you show me your work, we will also look at your neighbour's work too. Remember you have five minutes.'

You have made it clear but not in a confrontational manner that you are aware that student B has been copying from student A. You have given them a time warning which will indicate that they have the opportunity to rectify the situation.

After five minutes, you can ask to look at student A's work first and give this student some specific feedback. Then, you can then look at student B's work and by asking them questions you can check whether they have understood what they are doing. At this point, as you are having this one-to-one conversation with the student it is probably worth saying that copying student A's work is not going to help them and that asking you is the best policy in future. You can then give them a time limit for the rest of the writing activity, e.g. six minutes, and say that you want to see their work again in that time. Make sure you return to student B in that time limit and praise them for the work that they have completed without any copying.

The outcome should be that the student feels more confident about their ability to complete the task because of your intervention and your praise. However, if the student was copying because they couldn't be bothered to think of the ideas themselves, then you have shown them that you have recognised this issue and have dealt with it in a non-confrontational manner.

A student is eating during your lesson

You are talking to the whole class at one particular point during your lesson. You spot that a student is reaching into their bag and taking out a sandwich which they are taking bites out of when they think you are not looking.

WHAT DO YOU DO?

1 Continue to talk to the rest of the class and move to where the student is sitting and teach some of the lesson from this spot. Set the students an activity as quickly as possible and then talk to the student. Say '[Name of student] I have seen you eating in my lesson. Why are you eating in my lesson?' The student will come up with some excuse about being hungry, has not had any lunch etc. If they handle the conversation well and are apologetic then you just need to explain why they should avoid eating in your lesson again. '[Name of student] can you make sure you eat at lunch or break time etc. and not in my lesson? If you start eating in my lesson everyone will want to eat and then we will end up having a picnic in here rather than learning anything. I will let you off this time [name of student] but don't do it again.'

A little bit of humour will help to defuse the situation as well as reminding the student about the specific reason why they should not eat in your lesson.

In a humorous way you have also suggested a way they can avoid eating in your lesson in the future. This will then allow you to start the next lesson with a comment to the particular student along the lines of, 'Have you remembered to have lunch before my lesson today?' thus reinforcing the message that you have not forgotten what happened in the previous lesson and you are expecting the student to comply with the rules.

2 Stop what you are talking about and challenge the student, '[Name of student] you know that you are not meant to be eating in my lesson, it is against the school rules. Why are you eating? Put it away immediately and don't let me see that again.'

What has happened to the structure of your lesson? Who is everyone looking at? What happens if the student says 'It wasn't me, I wasn't eating.' Then what happens? Do you start saying 'Yes, you were eating, I saw you' etc. Will the student continue to deny it? Where is this going to end up? Are you going to have to do something more serious about the incident if the student continues to defy you? What has happened to the atmosphere of your lesson?

3 Walk over to the student while you are still teaching/talking and take the food away from the student if you can see it. However, the student might start to say 'You can't do that. Give it back. It is my food.'

You can tell the student that you are putting the food on your desk and that they can come and collect it at the end of the lesson and you will keep it in public view so they can be assured that you won't eat it or put it in the bin. However, when the student comes and collects the food at the end of the lesson, make sure you pick it up and hand it to the student so that he/she has to listen, as you tell him/her that eating in your lesson is not allowed. Next time you find the student eating in your lesson, you will put the food in the bin or put them in detention etc. (whatever is appropriate within your school context).

A student is refusing to do any work in your lesson

Students are in the learning phase of your lesson and are meant to be completing a written task. You have explained the task and checked for any lack of understanding etc. You are working your way around the class, offering support when you see that a particular student is not doing any work. This student has not opened their book etc. and is starting to distract others around them.

WHAT DO YOU DO?

1   You move to the student and bend down to their level and say to them 'How can I help you? What don't you understand?' The student is likely to say 'I don't understand any of it so I can't do it.' This is quite common for students who are trying to avoid doing any work.

However, as long as you are confident that the task is appropriate for the student's ability, it can be helpful to break down the task into much smaller chunks. For example, tell them to 'complete Question 1' or 'write three sentences' and indicate on the page about how much they should write. Putting a little star on the page to demonstrate the amount of work to complete tends to help. Be very clear that the student should complete this amount and that you will return in five minutes to see how much they have done. You MUST make sure that you return in that time span as you need to praise the student for whatever they have managed to do. You can then set them the next small part of the task to do within a strict time limit (or skip to another part of the task) and return to check their progress. Keep this process going for as long as needed. Ensure that you praise them for whatever they have achieved but set clear targets each time. Some students need to feel that they have your individual attention and this is fine as long as they contribute to the lesson in a positive manner by continuing to follow your instructions. As in (3) you also need to tell the student how they should behave when they are stuck next time.

Depending on the student, you may find it appropriate to praise them in front of the class when you are commenting on how well you think the class has done. It doesn't matter if the student has not completed as much as everyone else but DO NOT slow the pace of the lesson down to suit the working pace of that particular student.

2   You can move over to the student and say to them '[Name of student] I have explained the task to you. Do you need me to explain anything else? I suggest that you start the task otherwise you will be spending part of your break time/lunchtime with me and making up for the missed work. Right, thanks.'

You have now given yourself time to work with other students in the class but how have you ensured that the student is now working? Is the student likely to start work after that conversation? Is the threat of staying behind after the lesson going to be enough to persuade him/her to work? Are they likely to start to distract others in the room? Why would they do that? Is it because the student is bored? Is the work too easy or too hard? Could you now end up with a bigger behaviour management issue?

You are likely to have to escalate the sanctions if their low-level poor behaviour increases as the lesson develops. You may end up having to send the student out of the lesson. Do you think this might have been the student's intention all along? Sending the student out of the lesson will only have helped them to avoid doing any work in your lesson. How is the situation going to be different in the next lesson? What message are you sending to the other students about what happens to students who don't work in your lesson? Is it, if you don't work you can be sent out and still not do any work in the required lesson time? This will not be your intended message but you may find the way you handle this particular student will reinforce a 'non-working' culture with this particular class.

3   From where you are in the room you say '[Name of student] you are meant to be working on [name of task]. Can you get on with it. Thanks.' What happens if the student then says 'No, I won't as I don't understand it.' What do you do? What is starting to happen to everyone else in the classroom? Who are they looking at? What has the non-working student managed to achieve?

At this point, you need to move across to the student and give them a strategy to use when they don't understand next time instead of just not engaging with the work. You can say to them '[Name of student] next time you don't understand something, you need to put your hand up. Right, how can I help you?' By doing this you are giving the student a message about future behaviour but you are also maintaining a positive relationship with them by offering to help. This will also check that the student is really stuck and not just bored or simply choosing not to do the work.

A student is talking

You are in a teaching phase of your lesson, you are teaching the students so they should be silent and listening to you. However, while you are teaching you notice that there are two students who are talking while you are talking. You have tried staring at them and making it clear that you know that they are talking but this has not stopped them.

WHAT DO YOU DO?

1   Stop what you are saying and address the two students '[Names of students] you have been talking for about the last two to three minutes. You need to be listening to me while I am talking. I will be talking for the next four minutes. That is your first warning (or whatever is appropriate in the context of your school) and if you cannot remain silent for the next four minutes then I will move you immediately.'

Although the attention of the class is on the two students rather than you, you can be seen to be dealing with the problem within very clear guidelines. You have given the two students a choice to cooperate with you. You have given them specific instructions about how to improve their behaviour and a clear time limit about how long you expect the positive behaviour to last.

בעזהשי"ת

בסימן טוב ובמזל טוב

עוד ישמע בערי יהודה ובחוצות ירושלים

נעלה את ירושלים על ראש שמחתנו

בשבח והודאה להשי"ת שהחיינו וקיימנו והגיענו לזמן הזה

ובלב מלא שמחה מתכבדים אנו להזמין את כבוד קרובינו וידידינו

לבא להשתתף בשמחת כלולת בנינו היקרים

הכלה הבתולה המהוללה		הבחור החתן המופלג
ברכה תחי'	עב"ג	אפרים הלוי ני"ו

שתתקיים אי"ה למזל טוב

ביום החמישי לפרשת שופטים ה' אלול תשע"ה לפ"ק

בחצר ביהכנ"ס סטינקורט,

קבלת פנים בשעה 3.00   חופה בשעה 3.30

קבלת פני האורחים אחר החופה

שמחת חתן וכלה בשעה 10.30 באולם בית יוסף

ואי"ה בשמחתכם נשיב לכם כגמולכם הטוב

הורי הכלה	הורי החתן
יהושע הכהן יעקבסון ורעיתו	שמעון הלוי ליכטנשטיין ורעיתו
מנשסתר	ציריך

בעזהשי"ת

Mr and Mrs Peter Simon Lichtenstein
together with
Rabbi and Mrs Yehoshua Jacobson
are delighted to invite you to celebrate
the marriage of their dear children

Efraim
& Brocha

which will אי"ה take place on
Thursday 16th August 2018
at Stenecourt,
Holden Road, Salford M7 4LN
Kabolas Ponim at 3.00pm
Chupa at 3.30pm prompt
followed by Reception until 5.00pm
Simchas Chosson v'Kalloh at 10.30pm
at the Beis Yosef Hall
Bury New Road, Prestwich M25 0JW

We look forward to welcoming you at our Simcha

חתן

Uetlibergstrasse 22
8045 Zürich

כלה

4 Mowbray Avenue
Prestwich M25 0LP

Honoured Grandparents
Dr & Mrs R. Jacobson, Mr & Mrs M. Cohen

Behaviour in this context can be improved when you indicate how long you are going to talk for. Students tend to respond better when they have a clear time limit and it also allows you to be very specific in your feedback to them.

If the talking continues you can then say 'I told you quite clearly that I was only talking for another four minutes and you are clearly unable to cooperate with that. I would now like you to move to [place each of them next to another student].' Try to avoid sending them out of the room at this point. However, when you say the above, you do need to move close to the students and not speak to them from the front of the room.

2   Stop what you are saying and address the two students. '[Names of students] can you repeat to me what I have just said? Do you understand what I have been talking about?' This gives the students the opportunity to repeat what you have just said and can make everyone else in the class laugh etc. Where is everyone's attention at this point? Is it on what you have been saying? Are you going to lose track of what you have been saying? Are you going to have to recap what you have been saying? Is this kind of approach actually going to stop the students from talking and how long for? What are you going to do next? How many times are you going to interrupt the learning of others in the class?

3   If it is possible to ignore their talking for the last few minutes that you are teaching, then try to do so. When you have started the rest of the class on an activity, move to the two students and talk to them directly and quietly. You can say 'You were clearly talking during the last four minutes. I chose to ignore it as I wanted to teach the rest of the class. However, you know that I will not tolerate that kind of behaviour and I would like [name of student] to move to sit next to [name of other student].' It doesn't matter if there is not much space in the room – they can make a three on a table etc.

You then say 'You will stay there for the next ten minutes and work with the other two students. If you do the work and cooperate then I will consider letting you move back after ten minutes.' Again, this is giving the student the option to work with you and you have set very clear guidelines. You also need to ensure you make it clear to the student left behind that you expect them to work well for the next ten minutes otherwise their friend will not return.

By doing it this way you are being seen as dealing with the situation but not at the expense of the learning of the other students. By only moving the student for a short time, you avoid the 'It wasn't me Miss' or the 'Why do I have to move, I wasn't talking?' etc. This way you can tell them that they are only moving for ten minutes but you can make it longer if they continue to criticise your decision. (3) also works as an additional strategy after putting (2) in place.

EXTRA NOTE

Please note that ideally you should not talk to your students for more than ten minutes at any one time without setting them an activity to complete. It doesn't have to be a long activity but enough to give the students' brains a rest from listening and absorbing information from you. A lack of pace to activities in lessons can be one of the greatest causes of off-task behaviour from students.

A student is tapping a pen

You are in the teaching phase of your lesson and talking to the students. However, you can see and hear that a student is tapping their pen on the radiator or table while you are talking.

WHAT DO YOU DO?

1 Stop what you are talking about and say to the student '[Name of student] please stop tapping your pen, it is very irritating and disruptive to the others.' Where is the attention of all the students at this point – on you or the student with the pen? What do you think you have indicated by using the word 'please'? Are you telling the student to stop or asking them to stop? What have you also indicated to the student about the impact of what they are doing? Will they now feel that they have found something to irritate you with? How long do you think they are going to stop tapping for? Is there a possibility that other students might start, now they know the impact it has on you?

2 Carry on talking and move to where the student is and try to avoid eye-contact. Look like you are going to walk past the student but just reach across and gently remove the pen from their hand. Will the other students have really noticed what is happening? What is the pen-tapping student going to do? Have you solved the problem? Are they able to continue tapping their pen? If the student does say something like 'Hey Sir, that's my pen, you can't take my pen', just walk to the front of the room and say something quickly like 'We will talk about it in minute [name of student]' and carry on with what you are meant to be teaching. You can then return the pen to the student at a suitable moment in the lesson and remind them not to do it again.

3 Move to where the student is sitting and say to him/her 'Give me your pen. You have been tapping the radiator/table with it and you need to stop. Give me your pen.' You have had to interrupt what you are talking about to the rest of the students by saying this so everyone's attention will be on the pen-tapping student. What happens if the student then simply puts the pen in their pocket and says 'I've put it away. I won't do it again'?

If the student does put their pen away, you can say to them 'Well done, next time I hear you tapping it, I will take it away.' However, there is the possibility that they might start again once you have moved away but in this case, the best policy is to make eye contact with the student or ignore the tapping until you can talk to them while the other students are working.

Some students may not give you their pen when you tell them to do so. What do you do now? You have now escalated a low-level behaviour issue into something much bigger than you had intended. The best way to get yourself immediately out of that situation is to say '[Name of student] you either give me the pen or you stop tapping it. If you don't stop tapping it while I am still teaching then I will ask you to leave my lesson [or some other suitable choice for the context of your school].' This allows you to continue with the rest of the lesson as you have given the student a very clear choice and time limit. Once you have started the rest of the class on an activity, you should return to the student and talk about how not following your instructions is not something that you find acceptable in your lesson. Make it very clear what the consequences will be if they do not follow your instructions again. However, with particular students you need to avoid putting yourself in the position where they can defy you in the first place.

SCENARIO 8

A student is texting on their mobile phone during your lesson

A student is texting on their mobile phone when the student is meant to be working.

WHAT DO YOU DO?

1 You can walk over to the student and demand that they hand over their phone as it is against the school rules to have a mobile phone out in the lesson. What do you think might happen at this point? It might be easier to give them a choice which is to put the mobile phone away out of sight or you will confiscate it. If you remember to give them a choice then it should not turn into a confrontation.

However, you may wish to have a quick word with the student at the end of the lesson or some appropriate moment in the lesson to reinforce the fact that they shouldn't be using a phone in your lessons. You need to spell out quite clearly what will happen if you see the phone in another lesson. Keeping the student behind at the end of the lesson also reinforces the message to the other students that you have taken the issue seriously even though you may not have confiscated it in the lesson.

When you talk to the student you need to be very clear about what will happen if you see their phone in future lessons. You will either confiscate it or report the student to the appropriate member of staff. It may not be the correct form of action to take the phone from the student in a future lesson if you see it, as they may refuse to give it to you. However, you can show that you have dealt with it as long as you tell the student that, because they have refused to do as you had previously agreed, then you will take further action. You can tell them that this will be to refer it to member of staff, put the student in school detention etc. (whatever is appropriate for your school context). No need to give them a choice in the next lesson if they use their phone again as you have clearly told them what would happen if you saw it again. This stops it from becoming a 'game' for the student to see if they can interrupt your lesson, irritate you etc. by letting you see their mobile phone in subsequent lessons.

2 You can walk over to the student if you are talking to the class and carry on while you stand right next to them. What do you think the student will do at this point? They should put their phone away, which deals with the issue in the immediate context. However, at the appropriate point of the lesson, you can then speak to the student and remind them of the school rules and clearly spell out the consequences of their actions if you see their mobile phone again. Then refer to (1) for further guidance about how to deal with their phone if you see it in a future lesson.

3 You can stop what you are doing and demand that student hand over their phone as it is against school rules. You can then tell them how to collect their phone etc. depending on what your school context is. What do you think is likely to happen at this point? You will have to judge, depending on the student, how likely it is they will give you the phone if you demand for it in this manner.

A student leaves when you have sent them out

You have sent a student out of your lesson to wait in the corridor. You have done this because of the student's disruptive behaviour in your class. This is not the first time that this has happened. When you go out of the classroom (after about five minutes) to talk to the student, you find that they are not there.

WHAT DO YOU DO?

1 You can leave the door open to your classroom and monitor whether the student returns for about ten minutes. Be quite strict with this time limit as ten to fifteen minutes in total is probably sufficient time for the student to claim that they went to the toilet if they do return. If the student has not returned within ten minutes you should follow school procedure which would be to notify the School Office or another senior member of staff. You need to tell someone quickly for the safety of the student but also because you are meant to be in charge of this student but you no longer know where they are.

Hopefully once you have notified someone else the situation for the rest of the lesson will be taken out of your hands. However, if you get the chance (depending on the remaining length of the lesson) you might want to check whether anyone has found the student. If not, it might be appropriate to ask the student's classmates where they think the student might have gone but it is probably advisable to involve the rest of the class as the last resort.

Before the next lesson, you, the student and a senior member of staff need to meet and discuss this student's actions. You need to explain the impact that this student's behaviour is having on the rest of the class and the actions you have taken in the past. Do not be anecdotal with the information you give. Be specific with dates, the action you took and the reaction of the student. Comment on the student's behaviour rather than their personality. Being objective will demonstrate that you have been consistent in your approach and have taken all the appropriate action with this student. It should also strengthen your case if you feel that the student should be removed from your lessons for a period of time or permanently moved to another class.

2   Return back to the classroom and wait for ten minutes but spend that time gathering some work together that can be given to the student when they return (see (1) if student A does not return within ten minutes.) Try and put this work together even if it means that you have to stretch out an activity that you have asked the rest of the students to complete. In addition, depending on the context of your school, organise in your head where you can send the student when they return.

When student A returns, they are liable to attract attention to their return by opening the door and saying 'I'm back . . .' in order to make the rest of the students laugh. The student might start knocking on the door or shouting outside the room in the corridor. Try not to respond to their behaviour apart from making eye contact and state very firmly 'Outside [name of student].' Pick up the work that you have and take it outside. Say very little to the student and whatever you do say – do it in a calm and measured manner. It may be along the lines of '[Name of student] I do not expect you to go off by yourself during my lesson so I am now going to escort you to another lesson/office/corridor etc. as you clearly do not know how to behave in my lesson.' Try to avoid any other discussion and simply tell the student to follow you and take them to wherever you have planned. Ask the member of staff to collect the student's work at the end of the lesson and say that you will ensure that the student's belongings are taken to him/her before they leave. Essentially you want to avoid seeing this student at the end of the lesson.

Return to your class and explain that this student won't be returning for the duration of your lesson. A few minutes before the end of the lesson, ask one of the more trustworthy students to take student A's bag etc. to wherever they are. You now need to follow this incident up with a senior member of staff as soon as possible. This is not the type of incident that can wait till the next day. You need to tell your Head of Department/Head of Year etc. and explain what has happened. Read (1) to give you guidance about how to handle this meeting and the information that you need to include.

3   Carry on with your teaching and wait for the student to return – you may not wish to leave this for longer than ten minutes before you inform another member of staff. However, if the student returns and attracts attention to themselves, which they inevitably will, you can say something along the lines of 'Thank you [name of student] for returning to my lesson. I am pleased that you have managed to fit us in with your other pressing appointments. By my calculation, you have wasted fifteen minutes of my lesson so you will therefore make that time up at the end of my lesson/detention etc.' Break eye contact with the student and indicate that they should return to a new seat in the classroom.

You may have decided to move student A's books etc. to a new place in the classroom during their ten-minute absence in order to minimise disruption upon their return. Carry on working with other students and then after about five minutes go and talk to student A while the rest of the class is at work. Take this opportunity to tell student A that their behaviour has been inappropriate and that you will have to refer it to another member of staff. Keep your tone calm and measured and try not to engage with their excuses. Keep your responses short and factual. Explain that you had sent the student out of the classroom because they had done 'x' and during this time the student had disappeared without asking permission. This is breaking the school rules and therefore action needs to be taken.

However, keep your tone positive and explain that the sanctions are likely to be less if the student cooperates for the rest of your lesson. Try and include them in the lesson by explaining the work etc. and using praise sparingly if you think it is appropriate. If the student does not respond positively and continues to be disruptive, tell them to leave the classroom and escort them to another room immediately. Again, try to avoid seeing the student at the end of the lesson without a senior member of staff who can help you resolve the situation and impose some sanctions on this student's behaviour.

EXTRA NOTE

A variation on leaving your class to take student A to another classroom would be to ask a trusted student to take a note to the teacher next door/School Office etc. and ask them to come and collect student A. Make sure you still collate some work together and possibly the student's belongings too although you might ask one of student A's classmates to put things into student A's bag. Doing all these things will ensure that when student A returns, they do not step back into your classroom and your reaction to his/her return is measured and calm. You can tell student A to wait outside upon their return while you wait for the other member of staff to arrive. You may not wish to tell the student that this is the reason; instead tell him/her to wait until you choose for them to enter your classroom.

SCENARIO *10*

A student makes homophobic comments

You hear a student (A) making homophobic comments about another student (B) in the class.

HOW DO YOU HANDLE THIS SITUATION?

1 From where you are standing in the classroom say '[Name of student A] I heard what you just said about [name of student B]. I will not have that type of language in my classroom. Go outside in the corridor until I decide that I want you back in my lesson.' Your reaction does give a strong impression about your intolerance of this kind of language. However, what are the other students going to do at this point? Are they going to start to discuss what was said about student B? How is student B going to feel at this point?

What happens if student A says 'It wasn't me, it was [name of other student C], he/she was the one that called student B a *****.' The situation has now escalated and you have given a platform for student A to publicly call student B an inappropriate name. Your reaction at this point is likely to be 'I don't care – I will not tolerate that kind of language and you and student C will wait outside in the corridor.' At this point the rest of the class are likely to be laughing and student B is probably hoping that the floor will open and let them drop into it.

You will have to calm the situation down by moving round the classroom and using your physical presence and comments to focus the students back on their work. You may have to use some kind of sanction to settle some students down. Try to avoid paying too much attention to student B as he/she will not appreciate this at this point of time.

At some point, you are going to have to let students A and C back into the classroom or send them to another class, depending on the seriousness of the situation. Whatever you choose to do, you have to be prepared before you talk to them. You either need to take their pens, books and work outside to them or you may want to move their stuff to another desk in the room (you may have to move students around) before you go and talk to them. If you are keeping the students in the classroom then you might want to write down on a piece of paper the three expectations that you have of them when they arrive back in your lesson.

You need to keep the conversation short and calm otherwise it will end up being confrontational. You may simply tell the students that the type of language that was used was inappropriate and you will not tolerate it in your lesson. You will follow it up with other members of staff and tell them that they will be talking to you before the start of the next lesson. You need to be very clear about your expectations of their behaviour for the rest of the lesson. Break this down into three points and either give the points to them on paper or verbally tell them. An example could be:

- You will not talk about anyone else in the class.

- You will complete all work within the time limit that I set you.

- You will work by yourself and only talk to someone if directed by me.

You then let the students back in the classroom or send them to another class but because you have organised the work/desks beforehand this should be done with the minimum of disruption. You can then refer to the three points if you need to throughout the lesson and also employ sanctions if you feel that they have not fulfilled any of the expectations. This is much easier and avoids more confrontation if you have been very explicit about what they are, e.g. have written them down.

After the lesson, you need to talk to the students' form tutor or your Head of Department about how to handle this situation. Your school may have clear guidelines about the sanctions for this type of language. You or someone else needs to talk to the students before they return to your lesson. You may need to reissue the expectations or something similar for these students and use this as a Code of Behaviour for these students for future lessons.

You may also wish to talk to student B and find out what action they would like you to take about what happened. You might not want to do this at the end of that particular lesson as student B will not want to be singled out again. However, finding student B at some other time before your next lesson will give them the confidence that you are doing something about it and also give them the opportunity to discuss actions with you.

2 You can walk over to student A with a piece of paper and ask them to write down the word they have just used. Students sometimes think it is funny that you are allowing them to write it down so will do it. Other students will ask you why you are asking them to write it down but simply say that if student A can say a word out loud then surely they can write it down on a piece of paper. You then take the piece of paper and say 'Thanks [name of student] at break time I will show this to [name of senior member of staff] who will want to discuss with you why you were writing this sort of language down in my lesson.' Try to walk away and not engage with any further discussion other than to say 'OK [name of student A] focus on the lesson now and we will talk about it later.' This indicates that you are in control but at the same time it does show student A that they will have the opportunity to discuss their concerns with you later.

Your main immediate focus is to detract attention from the incident and continue with your lesson. You have shown that there is a consequence for bad behaviour but you don't want to focus on it any more for the sake of student B but also for the teaching and learning that needs to take place in your lesson. You will need to talk to student A about their concerns about you showing the piece of paper to a senior member of staff but this needs to be done at a time to suit you and not student A. You will have to decide how to handle this conversation depending on the type of student, whether you think it will happen again, and whether it is important for you to be seen to carry out the sanction with this student/class or the threat has been enough.

You must then show this piece of paper to a senior member of staff (if that is what you have decided to do) and you must emphasise to the member of staff how some kind of action needs to be taken before student A arrives for your next lesson. This is the type of incident that needs to be dealt with swiftly and your school context will determine how seriously it is taken.

3   '[Name of student] I heard what you just said. What makes you think that is an appropriate word to use in my classroom? Who were you talking about? Do you think that is the right word to use to describe someone? Do you actually know what it means? Do you know why I find it offensive?'

This approach will make student A reflect on the language they have used and it brings the issue into the open. It allows the students to discuss the taboo on homophobic language but you may find that you are asked questions that you are unsure how to handle. You will find that if you use the words and talk about them in an informative (rather than an emotional and personal) manner it can help to take away the shock value of saying the words aloud in your classroom. Students know that homophobic language is not tolerated in schools but they can be unsure of why. It is language that some students use consistently out of school and it needs to be explained to them why it is not suitable within a school or professional context.

Encouraging this type of discussion will depend on your relationship with the class and also the age of the students. You may feel that it is appropriate to discuss it with younger students who are perhaps 'trying out' the words to see what effect it has. However, older students know the effect that it has and are trying to see what you will do about it. This means that you should take a firm line about your tolerance level of it in your classroom and deal with it depending on the context of your school.

EXTRA NOTE

In all cases, the strategy you use depends on the impact that the homophobic language has had on the student who has been affected. Some schools have a zero tolerance policy on homophobic language and the actions you take will be determined for you. Other schools will take the view that it depends on the seriousness of the words and the impact it has had on an individual and this relies on your judgement within the context you find yourself in.

The act of writing the word down as in (2) helps to add weight to the use of the word. It is easy to deny the impact of a word when it is spoken but not when you see it written down. By asking the student to write the word down, you are asking them to reflect on the impact the word might have and how the use of it can affect other students, but ultimately them too, if you choose to refer it on to another member of staff.

Once this incident is over in your classroom you can then ask other members of staff about how they would deal with the same incident. Your school may have a set policy which you can clearly implement but (2) will get you out of an unexpected incident within one lesson.

SCENARIO *11*

A student refuses to work in a group

For the main activity of the lesson, you have organised the groupings of students so that they can create, discuss, debate or rank ideas on a particular topic. You inform the students of these groupings and they all start to organise themselves apart from one student (A) who says loudly 'I am not working in that group. I hate these groups. Why can't we work with our friends and why do you always make us work with people we don't like?'

WHAT DO YOU DO NOW?

1　From your position in the class say '[Name of student] there is no need for that kind of talk. You will go and work with the group I have told you to otherwise I will put you in detention. It is only for ten minutes and if you cannot work with that group then you will make up the time at lunchtime/end of school.' Have you escalated the situation by giving the detention as a choice? How is student A likely to react to this choice?

For some students this will be enough of a sanction but others will still not follow your request. What do you do now? There is also the possibility that there is a genuine reason for the student not wishing to work in the assigned group and your actions have just ensured that the student cannot tell you what they might be. At this point, students from the assigned group might start to join in and say that they don't want student A to work with them anyway. This then creates a rather difficult and unproductive situation which leaves you with students refusing to work in the groups that you have assigned. At this point, it might be necessary to send student A out of the classroom. Read (3) to demonstrate how the situation might be handled from that point forward.

2   Go and stand near student A and with your body language indicate that you will listen to them in a minute. From this place in the room, ensure that the other students are following your instructions and give them lots of individual praise for doing so. Is student A more likely or less likely to continue to talk loudly when you are standing next to them? By praising the students you are giving them a reason for not joining 'camp' with student A and the quickest way of doing that is by rewarding their cooperative behaviour with praise. Quickly check that each group is working and give them a clear time limit for the activity.

Then return to student A and point out how everyone else is working successfully in this activity and it is only for ten minutes. Give them a choice about working with their assigned group for ten minutes or spending the time with you doing a spelling test/marking books etc. Hopefully this use of humour within the choice and giving them a specific time limit for their group work will make them cooperate. At this point, you may also wish to tell the student that talking to you in that manner was inappropriate and you do not wish for that to be repeated. Break eye contact with the student and move away to give them the opportunity to comply with your request.

If student A does not join the group then you will have no choice but to implement your sanction of making them complete a quick spelling test. However, before you do this you might want to say 'Sorry, I forgot to mention that with the choice of the spelling test/marking books etc. is a ten-minute detention at lunchtime [or whatever is appropriate for your school context].' This should ensure that the student complies with your request to work with the group. When the student does join the group, leave it for a few minutes and then walk over to give the whole group some praise.

Have you attracted the attention of the rest of the class by your actions? Have you clearly rewarded the good behaviour rather than publicly commenting on the bad behaviour? Have you given the student a choice to engage with the right behaviour?

3   You can send the student out for talking to you in a disrespectful manner which then gives you the opportunity to ensure that the rest of the students do work in their groups. Praise the students for working in a positive manner but try to keep the praise specific rather than too general as that can sound patronising depending on the age of the students.

After a few minutes, talk to student A outside and find out what the problem is. There may be a genuine reason for student A not working with other students. However, you will have to use your knowledge about the student to judge how authentic you think their point is. If you let the student work in another group then what message does it send to the other students? Could other students refuse to work in their groups? What will happen to the learning of the lesson if students end up not working in their groups?

You may find reminding the student that the task is only for ten minutes is probably the best way to ensure their cooperation as the student is more likely to join the group if they think it is for a short period of time. However, once the student has worked with the group for ten minutes, it is quite easy to start the next activity with student A still within the group. Giving student A praise for their contributions to the group work will also help to maintain their cooperation.

EXTRA NOTE

You may find a technique to avoid this type of behaviour from students when working in groups is to organise two types of group work seating plans. One seating plan is for collaborative and creative discussion – 'talk partners' (i.e. friendship groups) and the other seating plan is for more analytical/investigative discussion 'learning partners' (i.e. mixed ability groups/same ability groups etc.). Giving these groupings a theme/colour etc. makes them much easier to organise, as you can display the code word at the start of the lesson and as the students enter the room they can seat themselves accordingly. It also helps you to quickly mix up the group work within a lesson if you wish to, as the students can easily move from their creative discussion to a more analytical one with the minimum amount of fuss.

A student swears in your lesson

You hear a student swearing in your lesson. The student does not swear at you but you hear them using swear language in a conversation with another student.

WHAT DO YOU DO NEXT?

1   Walk over and stand close to the student and say calmly and quietly that you don't expect to hear that kind of language in your classroom. Your classroom is a learning environment and as swearing is not tolerated in other situations, it is not allowed in your classroom. You can then explain that if this student chooses to swear again in your lesson you will ask them to leave. Ask them if they understand. What do they need to say now? Hopefully, they will apologise and you can walk away and carry on with working with other students.

Even if, during this conversation, the student denies that they said anything, you are having a conversation with just them and the whole class is not involved. You have not directly used their name or confronted them about it so it allows you to say 'You may not have said it but I thought I heard it coming from over here. However, I thought I would remind you what will happen if I hear any more swearing in my lesson.'

2 Shout '[Name of student], I heard that and it is not appropriate in my classroom. I will not have students using swear words in my classroom and I would like you to leave and wait for me outside in the corridor where we can discuss it further. Thanks.'

Some students may cooperate with your instructions but whether they do or not, everyone in the class now knows what has happened and who has done it. As the student is now the focus of attention, are they more or less likely to cooperate with you? As everyone is now looking at them, they are probably going to say that it was not them and they didn't say it etc. You will end up having to say that you did hear it and that you have asked them to leave and you want the student to follow your instruction. This is now likely to become a confrontation which could have been avoided and depending on the student and the class, may end up with the student leaving or not.

If the student will not leave, you may need to go and ask for another teacher to remove them from the lesson. If you have issued the ultimatum that they have to leave – whether your reason for doing this proves to be right or wrong – it will be difficult to keep the student in the lesson from the standpoint that they are clearly defying you.

3 You can walk towards the student saying '[Name of student] did I hear you say something? Is there something you wish to share with me? I didn't hear you use a swear word, did I? No, I didn't think so. We don't use that type of language in my lesson, do we? Right, didn't think so. Make sure I don't hear it again. Thanks.' You can then move away and work with other students for a while.

By using a little bit of humour, you have defused the situation but have not directly accused the student. However, you have publicly and within the hearing of other students, established the fact that use of swear language is not appropriate in your lesson. By asking them a series of rhetorical questions, you are asking them for their compliance but in a non-confrontational manner.

You may wish to talk to this student later on in the lesson and praise them for whatever they have achieved at this point. This will maintain the positive relationship between you and give the student the opportunity to talk to you about the incident if they wish. For example, deny that it was them etc. This will allow them to share any frustration they might have with being talked to in such a public manner.

EXTRA NOTE

If a student does swear directly at you then allowing them to stay in the classroom is not an option. You need to ask them to leave and suggest that they are clearly angry and need a 'cooling-off' period. Keep your voice calm and measured. You don't need to shout at them or tell them using that type of language is inappropriate etc. The student knows that and shouting at them is likely to make their exit more dramatic as they might swear at you again before they leave.

You need to alert another member of staff who will hopefully deal with the student for the rest of the lesson for you, as you need to keep your contact with this student for the duration of this lesson to a minimum. However, you must talk to this student before the next lesson. You should do this with a more senior member of staff or form tutor etc. You need to try and find out the reason for the swearing as this cannot be a regular occurrence. If you think that the student is likely to swear at you again for whatever reason, you will need to talk to your Head of Department about moving this student to another class or another type of sanction.

It may be that your school has a more severe view about a student swearing at a teacher and once you have reported this incident then all of the above might be taken out of your hands. However, if there is the chance that the student will return to your lesson at any point in the future, you do need to try and find out what the reason might have been for the swearing. Knowing the reason is probably the only way that you and the student can avoid it happening again.

SCENARIO *13*

A student talks back to you in front of the other students

You have asked a student to stop talking while you are teaching the class and they have replied 'It wasn't me. You are always picking on me. I'm not the only one that talks, other people do, you don't tell them off though do you?'

HOW ARE YOU GOING TO HANDLE THIS SITUATION?

1   Your reply could be '[Name of student] you clearly feel that there is an issue to discuss here and I suggest we do it in a minute when I have finished explaining what I want everyone to do. Right, everyone listening to me and as I was saying . . .'

Without hesitation, you should carry on with what you were saying but you might need to cut short what you were intending to talk about so that you can quickly set the rest of the class on an activity which will enable you to talk to the student. You are indicating the expected behaviour but not singling out the particular student again. If this student does not comply with this instruction then they are choosing not to and are deliberately defying you. It is probably advisable to take more direct action at this point: for example, asking the student to leave the classroom and saying that you will talk to them out there. See (3) for a possible method to follow once you have sent the student out of the classroom.

If the student does not interrupt you any more then once you have set up the task for the other students you need to talk to this student straight away. You might want to start with 'Right, [name of student] we have two minutes to discuss what you said to me and work out what is going on.' It is sometimes advisable to give a time limit because if the conversation looks like it is going to carry on for too long or becomes too negative, you can stop it and tell the student that it is over the two minutes and that you can continue the conversation at the end of the lesson etc.

While talking to the student you should try asking them to reflect on whether they handled the situation correctly by interrupting you. How else could they have done it? What did they want to say? What do they think should be done about the fact that they feel you pick on them? By asking a series of questions, you are making the student reflect on their behaviour and by doing this you are also indicating that you are taking their points seriously.

However, you are also showing them that there are consequences to behaving inappropriately in your classroom. They cannot just say what they feel like at the time and disrupt others. They have to be able to support their points otherwise they are deliberately misbehaving and other sanctions can take place. By asking questions, you are also giving them the opportunity to feel that they are being consulted in further action rather than you imposing a course of action. With most students, the act of answering the questions makes them realise the inappropriateness of their behaviour whilst also giving them the opportunity to make amends.

However, this type of conversation can highlight certain things that you might not wish to be heard within the classroom. Depending on the student and the context, you might want to delay it until after the lesson. You need to tell the student that this is what is going to happen and for the rest of the lesson, you expect them to cooperate with the expected behaviour in your classroom. If they do not do this then you might want to look at sending them out of your classroom.

2 You can reply to the student directly with something along the lines of, 'Now, that isn't true is it? You were talking and I have already discussed this with you. It isn't the first time you have done this and you know it is not acceptable to talk while I am talking. I am sorry you feel this way and if you have a problem with me and the lesson then we need to discuss it but not right now. Right, as I was saying before I was rudely interrupted . . .'

This approach shows that you are dealing with the situation with respect and consideration and may be successful with some classes. However, you are apologising to the student for commenting on their poor behaviour. You are also giving them the opportunity to make further points in front of the other students. If you allow this exchange to continue between you and this student, you may end up feeling that you have no other option than to ask them to leave the class. This will inevitably undo any of the positive feelings that you might have been trying to create by treating their comment with respect at the start.

3   You can shout at the student and tell them to leave the classroom as you won't be talked to in that way. This does assert your authority and shows the other students that you will deal with behavioural issues in a direct manner. However, it doesn't solve the underlying issue. Does the student have a point? Do you think you focus your negative comments on a small number of students in the class? Do you praise good behaviour from this student when you spot it or is it only the negative behaviour that you comment on?

You can talk to the student outside the classroom at a suitable moment. It tends to be easier to have a frank conversation when there is not an audience of other students. You need to give the student very clear targets about your expectations in order to help them enter the classroom and allow you to teach them in a positive way. It may be that you need to allow the student (for only a few minutes) to give their point of view about your attitude towards them. Try not to engage with this and avoid defending your actions.

Listen and then state the short-term targets that you wish the student to follow in order to return to the classroom. You may find that it is helpful to jot these down on a piece of paper to give to the student so there is no misunderstanding about your expectations. For example, you will expect the student to:

* change seats and sit next to [name of another student]
* complete a specified amount of work in ten minutes
* remain silent while you are talking etc.

Also explain to them what will happen if they don't follow these targets in this lesson. Praise them for their cooperation with you and then allow them back in the classroom. Distract the other students in the classroom by attracting their attention or working with some of them as the student re-enters the classroom. Don't stand there and watch as the student walks in and moves places etc. Try and give the student the opportunity to follow your targets and engage in positive behaviour. If the student does not comply with your targets then you will need to state more sanctions in order to improve their behaviour. However, as soon as you see any positive behaviour from that moment on in the lesson, you must praise it instantly either publicly or privately, depending on the student.

EXTRA NOTE

It is very easy to comment on the negative behaviour you see students exhibit, which is where the comment 'you always pick on me' will have derived from. On reflection, you may feel that the student does have a point. You need to comment on the positive behaviour of all your students within every lesson and preferably on an individual basis. The amount and quantity of praise depends on the context. It is too easy to not comment on what you consider to be expected levels of good behaviour. However, the students can only meet your expectations for behaviour if you are explicit about them. Some of them will always fail if they are aiming for a picture of behaviour that is only in your head and has not been shared on a regular basis.

Students are passing notes

While you are teaching the class, you can see two students passing notes across the room. Other students are having to help to pass the notes.

WHAT DO YOU DO?

1   While you are talking, move next to one of the students who are passing notes and continue what you are saying from that spot. Is that student likely to continue passing notes at this stage? Have you interrupted your lesson? Is the attention still on you rather than the students? Have you given the students a choice at this stage? If they continue to attempt to pass notes, then stopping your lesson and giving them some kind of sanction for their behaviour is appropriate.

2   Walk around the room while you are talking and try to catch the notes as they are passed around the room, taking it off one of the student's desks. You can threaten to read the note but this is not advisable. Instead, you might want to acknowledge that you know it is a note and it is not appropriate to pass these around the room. You then put it in the bin. You can then also make clear what the sanction will be if you see another note.

3   Stop what you are saying and shout the names of the students and tell them to stop passing the notes. Tell the students that you have seen them pass notes three or four times and that they need to stop immediately. The students are likely to deny doing anything and may talk back to you. What do you do at this point? What has happened to your lesson? Who are all the students looking at? Are you able to prove that they have passed the notes? Can you see the notes at this stage? Now they know they have caught your attention, are they likely to continue passing the notes when you start talking to the class again?

EXTRA NOTE

You might want to think about why the students feel that they can pass notes around the room. Is it because you haven't established a 'pens down and facing the front' culture in your classroom while you are talking? Are you talking too much and are the students bored? You might find that if you address a couple of these points, then students passing notes during your lesson might not arise.

SCENARIO 15

A student is sitting in your chair

You are in the middle of your lesson and turn around from what you are doing in your lesson and find a student sitting in your chair saying 'This chair is nice and comfy. Why don't we get chairs like this? I like this chair. Why can't I have this one?'

WHAT DO YOU DO?

1   You laugh and make some kind of joke along the lines of 'Well, I need a comfy chair for my old bones/long legs/tired brain . . . When you have those you will be able to have a comfy chair like me. Can you now get off it as these old bones etc. need to sit on it? Thanks.'

What have you managed to maintain in this exchange? What have you also explained and how have you managed to assert your status? The use of 'thanks' but not 'please' helps to ascertain your status. You have used humour to help maintain the relationship and you have given some kind of explanation for the reason for the difference in the quality of the chairs. You have also not used sarcasm as you could have, by suggesting that you have earned the right to sit on the chair by becoming a teacher and the student will never do that unless they do some work and not sit on your chair.

2   You can ignore the student and carry on working with other students in the classroom. Your intention for doing this would be that if the student doesn't get any reaction then it won't be any fun. However, what do you do if they start to mimic you? Pretend that they are teaching the rest of the class? Read material on your desk? Mess with the electronic equipment?

If this happens, you may wish to walk up to them and have a quiet word about how if this behaviour continues then certain sanctions will take place. Try and give them a choice but essentially you need them to get off the chair as at this point they will have the class's attention.

3   '[Name of student] that is my chair and you should not be sitting on it. You need to get off it now.' What do you think is going to be the reaction of the student? Who is everyone going to be looking at? Is this going to affect how the student reacts to you? What happens if they ignore you and carry on talking to their friends or looking at things on your desk? What do you do now?

You can give the student a choice at this stage, which is to get off your chair or they will have to talk to you at the end of the lesson about the work they have missed as by sitting on your chair they are not doing what everyone else is. You can use humour at this point by suggesting that the student should get off your chair or they have to teach the rest of the lesson. However, this can be problematic as some students will say that they do wish to teach the rest of the lesson and this inevitably creates problems. Teaching the rest of the lesson or marking work etc. is not always the threat to some students that you might hope it would be.

Students who are absent on a regular basis

A student (or small group of students) is always absent for one of your lessons during a week or a fortnight. This is because they are given extra support in literacy, numeracy, have work experience etc. However, this means that the student/s are less engaged in your lessons, their behaviour can be disruptive at a low level and they are not up to date with the work. Assume that this withdrawal lesson is timetabled so it is not going to change.

HOW DO YOU HANDLE THIS SITUATION?

1 You can print off Powerpoint™ presentations, photocopy the work of (attending) students in the class and give this to the students who were absent to help fill in the gaps. However, this does not mean that they will engage with the work or make any sense of it. You could alter your seating plan so the (absent) students sit with some of your more able students who could help them out with the work, but this means giving time in the lesson for the more able students to explain the missed work to the (absent) students.

One way of doing this is at the start of the next lesson to divide the class into about five groups. Place the (absent) students within each of these groups. Give the rest of the (attending) students clear guidance about what you want them to tell the (absent) students (this can be from a 'hint' sheet, using the Powerpoints™ from last lesson etc.) and encourage the students to 'peer teach' each other. You may want to ensure that each member of the group takes turns in contributing to this by telling them there will be a short quiz that all of them to need to pass. This should take about five to six minutes of your lesson and can act as a starter as you are able to check whether the (attending) students can articulate the learning from the previous lesson and the (absent) students are learning the information from their peers.

Ask the students to return to their usual seating plan and ensure that the (absent) students are not grouped together. Then give the class a short quiz to complete about the learning from last lesson. You will need to decide whether there are rewards associated with success in the test or not. By stating that there will be a quiz on the topic you will have raised the status of the quality of the learning that you wanted to take place within the class and you should generally be pleased with the results. It will also have had the effect of involving all the students in the activities so that the (absent) students feel less alienated and the (attending) students will feel that their learning has been valued and shared. Finally, on another plus point, the students will have been organising the learning and teaching of this early part of the lesson instead of you.

2 You can create extension work for the rest of the class while you work with the small group of (absent) students. The benefits of the extension work for the rest of the class are that it will help deepen and strengthen their understanding and develop their independent learning skills. Again, for the extension work to be meaningful, it will need to have an outcome that is going to be shared with the rest of the class which will therefore increase the quality of the learning. You may find it easier if you differentiate the outcomes for the extension work and organise the groups beforehand. In this way the work is targeted at the ability range of the students. This will mean that fewer students will be off task and there are likely to be fewer incidents of off-task behaviour.

This will allow you to work with the (absent) students and help bring them up to speed with the work that has been missed. You may need to give them notes etc. to help speed up the learning in this session. You could also include the topics for the extension tasks and ask them to make notes on these when the (attending) students are doing their presentations. This will encourage the (absent) students to take an active role during the presentations of the other students. Alternatively, you may wish to organise an independent writing activity during this session which will allow you to leave the (absent) students and check on the progress of (attending) students. How much time you plan to allocate to this type of activity depends on the size of the class, the length of your lesson and whether or not the students are used to this type of work. If it is the first time, you may feel that you should only plan an extension activity for twenty minutes plus the feedback/presentation time.

Encouraging the students to make notes about each other's presentations in some kind of diagrammatic form, e.g. Venn diagrams, mind maps, learning maps, will help them to internalise the material as well as help you monitor the learning that has taken place.

In an ideal world, having a teaching assistant in the room would improve considerably the success of these types of activities.

3   Another strategy might be to plan the lesson that the (absent) students are not attending as your skills/extension work/masterclass lesson. You could plan activities that develop specific skills and not continue with the scheme of work in a linear fashion. This could be a problem if you are under pressure for time but (1) and (2) are also taking time out of your future lessons in order to help the (absent) students to catch up.

You could organise an extra masterclass for the (absent) students and, if possible, use electronic resources as the 'carrot' to encourage them to attend. It could be straight after one of their lessons with you for about twenty minutes. You could use class notes, Powerpoints™, students' work (which the (absent) students could access from a computer). If you have a school reward policy then encouraging some of the (attending) students (for rewards) to help with this masterclass would be of mutual benefit to all.

You could write a blog about the learning that took place in the lesson or encourage some of your other students to do this. While the (attending) students are doing a short activity at the start of the lesson, you can ask your (absent) students to read the blog and follow any links in order to catch up with the learning that took place in the missed lesson.

EXTRA NOTE

All the of the above are suggestions to help the students who have been absent feel included in the lessons. Their boredom or disengagement are the factors that are going to cause you low-level disruptive behaviour problems and some of the above strategies might help you to avoid this situation. Most of the strategies encourage the (attending) students to act in some kind of role as a 'peer teacher' which allows you to act in a more supportive role so that you and all of your students feel that something new has been gained from the lessons.

CHAPTER 3

MANAGING THE BEHAVIOUR OF STUDENTS AS YOUR LESSON DRAWS TO A CLOSE

What do you do when a student ...

A student does not contribute significantly to a group's presentation

A student is working in a group which has been asked to deliver some sort of presentation to the rest of the class by the end of the lesson. When it is this group's turn to share their ideas with the rest of the class, it becomes clear that student A has contributed a minimal amount to the group and has said hardly anything during the presentation.

HOW DO YOU HANDLE THIS SITUATION?

1 Praise the students in the group but be very specific with your praise and make it as individual as possible. For example, '[Name of student] you clearly picked up on the key words and ideas of this task as you did really well when you used the terms "x" and "y".' When you come to student A you could use sarcasm and say '[Name of student] – well, anything I say about your contribution is going to use more words than you did in the whole presentation. Thank you and we will talk about this further.' The other students in the class are likely to laugh at your comment.

Have you indicated your displeasure at student A's actions? Is the use of sarcasm appropriate here? Does it depend on the student? Do you need to be confident that the student understood the task and *chose* not to contribute rather than *not being able to* contribute to the task?

2 Praise the students in the group and be very specific with your praise – see (1). Then make eye contact with student A and ask them why they did not say anything. Did they understand? Did the rest of the group not help them? Having seen the other groups, do they think that their contribution was of the same quality?

How is student A going to react to these questions being asked so publicly? Are you going to get any genuine feedback from them about the task? Is the student going to be able to reflect on their behaviour genuinely if you talk to them in this manner? You can only be talking to student A like this in order to highlight their lack of contribution, but isn't this already obvious? If you have rewarded the positive behaviour correctly then you shouldn't need to highlight the negative behaviour in this way. Do you think you are going to prevent student A from behaving like this again? Is student A more or less likely to join in group work after this incident?

3 Praise the students in the group and be very specific with your praise – see (1). Discuss the learning points from this group work activity and end your lesson in the usual manner. While the students are packing up, walk over to student A and ask him/her to stay behind and talk to you. Talk to student A in an appropriate place (in the classroom with the door open/office/library etc.) and ask them for some genuine feedback about how they found that particular task. You don't need to indicate how poor you thought their contribution was as he/she will be aware of that. Ask similar questions to those in (2) but you are more likely to receive genuine answers at this point.

You will then need to spell out for student A how to behave when faced with a similar situation in group work. For example:

- Ask you for help if they don't understand
- Explain to you how they don't like talking in front of people and ask for a suggestion about how they can still contribute to the group
- Be given a very clear role within the group which can clearly be assessed

Some students genuinely don't like giving presentations but the student must be given strategies to deal with it and gain confidence in this area. Explaining the options that students have to assist them to deal with this issue can help considerably and it might help you be more informed about placing the student when organising groups in the future.

EXTRA NOTE

You may find that being very specific about the roles within group work will also help to prevent other students from having to 'carry' an uncooperative student. There are lots of methods for implementing roles within group work that you could investigate further. Defining the group roles can also help to make the contributions assessable which can be important in some subjects.

SCENARIO 2

A student ruins another student's work

It is towards the end of the lesson and students have been working for a period of time on a specific piece of work.

All of a sudden, student (A) shouts out 'I can't believe you have just done that. Miss/Sir, [name of student] has just wrecked my work. What do I do now? It is ruined! I have just spent all lesson on that . . . Miss/Sir, what are you going to do about it?'

HOW ARE YOU GOING TO HANDLE THIS SITUATION?

1 Walk over and say to student B '[Name of student] leave the classroom now. You have clearly ruined student A's work and we will talk about it at the end of the lesson.'

Student B will hopefully leave the classroom after you have told them to do so but they will probably say 'It wasn't me. I didn't mean to and see what Student A has been doing to my work all lesson. It's not fair. They've been messing up my work all lesson too.' You still need to repeat your instruction and ask them to leave.

This then gives you some breathing space to find out what has been going on. However, you need to think about how much of your lesson you have left as you might need to discuss the issue with both students at the end of the lesson. Student B could have deliberately ruined Student A's work to cause disruption to your lesson and put some attention on themselves for whatever reason. Sometimes, students ruin other students' work in order to hide their feeling of incompetence as they perceive their piece of work as not being of the same standard. They use the incident as a way of distracting attention from their work and causing disruption to your lesson etc.

You need to talk quickly and calmly to student A and reassure them that it is not the end of the world etc. However, you need to ensure that your lesson is ended in the usual orderly and reflective manner and focus on the other students.

2   Walk over to both students, telling student A to calm down for a minute. Look quickly at both students' work, make a judgement about whether the work has been 'ruined' or whether you can see evidence that student B's work has also been drawn on etc. If you feel that student A has come off worse but student B's work has also been drawn on, it is probably best to ask them both to leave the lesson where they can calm down for a minute. If you think student B is the main culprit then it is probably best to ask them to leave the room but without shouting. You can be very clear in your reason about why they need to leave as you can refer specifically to what you can see and point out that it is not acceptable. Again, when you ask both students to leave, if you have inspected their work then you can be very specific in your reasons for why they should leave.

You can then turn your attention to the rest of the class and ensure that the lesson finishes in the usual reflective and orderly manner. You may also take the opportunity to find out from other students what they think happened. Other students are more likely to talk to you about the incident if students A and B are out of the room.

When the rest of the class has gone you will find it easier to talk to either student B or both students. When talking to just student B you need to find out the reasons for his/her behaviour. You need to ask why they did it. There is no need to shout at student B as they know that they have done something wrong but you need to emphasise the impact that their behaviour has had on student A. You need to be very specific about what you have seen on the work and the damage that this has done. You then need to be very clear about the sanctions that you are going to impose (depending on the seriousness of the incident and the context of your school). It could be that the matter is referred to the Head of Department, the student is put into detention (during detention, you might suggest that they use the time to write a letter of apology to student A) or student B is removed from your class for a couple of lessons.

When you are talking to student A and student B, you need to very specific about what you have seen on both of their work. You might also mention the information that you have been given by the other students. You need to make it clear that you don't expect this kind of behaviour and ask why they thought drawing on each other's work was appropriate. Emphasise that you do not appreciate your lesson being disrupted in the way it was by student A shouting and then student B's reaction. For that reason, they will not sit together for the next two lessons (if they are friends) and/or they are in a detention (or something similar).

Sometimes, if they are good friends, students A and B can start laughing at this stage, which is why it is important to have this conversation at the end of the lesson. You don't want them returning to the lesson, laughing about what has been said by you outside the classroom and marginalising the situation to the other students. If student A is now not particularly bothered about what has happened as they thought it was a 'bit of a joke', then you may feel it is right to impose another appropriate sanction, explaining that it is because they have caused you to spend extra time with them when it is not necessary. Again, that is why it is important to send them out so you are not spending time with them instead of the well-behaved students who are in your lesson.

In both cases, talking to student A and/or student B in a factual manner by referring to what you have seen on the work is a more successful approach. This helps to depersonalise the issue as you are dealing in factual points. However, student B does need to realise the impact that their behaviour has had on student A (if applicable) so asking them to empathise is appropriate. At no point should you have commented on student B as a person e.g. by suggesting they were stupid, naughty or immature. You should have kept your comments specifically about the behaviour and used more impersonal language, which helps to defuse any tension that might exist between you and ensure that the situation ends in an appropriate manner.

3   Walk over and say to student B '[Name of student] why have you done that? What is the purpose of that? See how upset student A is! This is a serious matter and while I talk to student A about this, I need you to leave the classroom. We will talk about it more at the end of the lesson.'

At this point, you have not really given yourself time to investigate what the 'ruined work' looks like plus by your language and reaction, you have also escalated the situation. Student B is not going to react very well to being told to leave the classroom in this manner and is likely to be more disruptive on the way out. Student A could 'play up' to your reaction and exaggerate what has happened; for example, start crying, start swearing, being very negative towards you and the situation. The whole class is now watching and listening to what is going on plus you have to talk to student A and try to find out what has happened.

You may also find out when you examine the work that it is not ruined but there has only been a clear attempt to draw a line/mark on it etc. However, equally it could be ruined and then it is a serious incident depending on the importance of the work. It is also useful to look at student B's work too and see if you can see any evidence of any kind of graffiti on their work in case their point about student A having done it too is true. If you think this is the case, you might wish to refer to (2) to see how to deal with that situation.

You now need to give some solutions to student A, which might be to photocopy someone else's work for them to have for next lesson (if that is appropriate). You don't have to be too specific at this point about the options because if student A is genuinely upset then they are not going to listen to much of what you are saying. Explain that you will also talk to student B and the necessary sanction will take place depending on your school's context. You need to say to student A that you can talk about this more at the end of the lesson. You could suggest leaving the lesson for a short time to calm down but ask them to return by the end of the lesson.

You should then walk away and turn your attention to the others in the class and end your lesson in the usual orderly manner. If student A is genuinely upset at this point, nothing you are going to say or do at this stage is going to help much so you need to focus on the other students. At the end of the lesson, if this a serious matter, you do need to ask student A what options they think you have in helping them to resolve the issue. Sometimes, asking the student to engage with the solutions helps them to feel involved with the process, especially if they haven't liked any of your suggested options, e.g. photocopying someone else's work. You also need to ensure that you listen to them and reassure them that something will be done.

Before the next lesson or even the next day, you should try and talk to student A about the situation again. This does depend on the seriousness of the case, e.g. is it GCSE coursework etc.? If you believe it is a serious issue then you need to tell your Head of Department and discuss the options. When you meet with student A before the next lesson, you might also wish to have your Head of Department with you so that the student realises that you have taken it seriously and that the options being given are ones that are supported by the Head of Department. This will help to defuse the situation and ensure that Student A cooperates with you in future lessons.

However, you may wish to ensure that student B is moved away from student A in future lessons. Again, you should try and inform student B of this move before the next lesson as this will help to defuse any more conflict at the start of the lesson. The rest of the students will also gain confidence in you by the fact that you have clearly dealt successfully with the situation as they are now not faced with another potentially disruptive incident in their next lesson with you.

A student writes graffiti on the desk

At the end of the lesson as you are walking around collecting resources etc. you notice that there is graffiti on one of the desks where one of your more difficult students is sitting. You know that there was no graffiti on the desks before the lesson.

WHAT DO YOU DO NOW?

1 Say '[Name of student] have you written this graffiti on here? That is not acceptable. What does it suggest about your attitude if you are writing on desks? These desks were clean this morning and you are the only one that has been sitting here. You are going to have stay here and clean it off. Who else do you think is going to clean it?'

The student is going to deny that it was them at this point. By handling this situation in this manner, you are clearly making a statement about your attitude towards graffiti and stating that there is a consequence for the student's actions. However, you could also end up in a confrontational dialogue as the student will deny it was them and you will say it was – these comments can go back and forwards for a while. The rest of the students will all now be listening and watching the outcome.

There is also the possibility that the student will finally say 'Think what you want. It wasn't me and I am not cleaning it.' He/she will then leave the classroom in a disruptive manner.

Do not attempt to go after the student or shout at them as he/she will not return to the room at this stage. Keep calm and say to the rest of the students that it looks like student A will be doing some cleaning in their own time. You then need to end the lesson in the usual orderly manner.

You need to immediately let someone senior know that student A has left your classroom without your permission. This could be your Head of Department/Head of Year etc. There is the possibility that student A will not attend their next lesson and other staff need to be aware that this could happen. You also need to take advice from your Head of Department about how you handle this situation with student A before the next lesson.

The graffiti needs to be cleaned off as soon as possible and this probably means that student A will not be doing it. If you cannot clean the graffiti off before your next class arrives then you need to mention it to the next student sitting at that desk. You should say that you are aware of the graffiti and that a student will be cleaning it off in their own time (this might not be the complete truth) and that you hope it is not made any bigger by the end of the lesson. You might want to check that more has not been added by the end of the lesson. Not acknowledging the graffiti in any way could mean that the students will think that it is acceptable to draw/write on your desks and this will also indicate to them that you do not value their learning environment.

2 Say to student '[Name of student] what's this on the desk? It wouldn't be something written by you would it? Don't tell me that you have been so excited about the content of today's lesson that you decided to write on the desk as well? I am impressed that you feel that you can make such an overwhelming contribution to my lesson but it is unfortunate that it is on the desk. Now that I have seen it and complimented you on your writing – what about I get you a cloth and you clean it off for me? Thanks.' At this point you smile and walk away. Quickly go and locate a cloth; if you can't sometimes another piece of paper with water on it will do the trick. Return to the student with a smile. Put the cloth on their desk and say 'Thanks for doing that.' Again, walk away quickly.

By doing it in this manner you are attempting to handle the situation with a bit of humour and you are also indicating that you are expecting the student's compliance by saying 'thanks' and walking away. You are not being confrontational but you are also not giving the student an opportunity to discuss it with you. Most of this conversation should have gone unnoticed by the other students and student A will hopefully comply with your request. The student might not clean it off very well and it is up to you how far you insist on the cleanliness. You should bear in mind that the student's success rate is going to depend on the equipment that you have given them as damp paper is not going to clean much off.

3 You can say nothing but simply go and get some cleaning cloths etc. – make sure there is enough for anyone else close enough to have been able to write the graffiti. Walk back to the desk and hand over the cleaning stuff. Say 'I am pretty sure that there was no graffiti on this desk this morning. I don't know who wrote it and I don't particularly want to read it. However, it needs to be cleaned off and if you all take collective responsibility for it then it will all be done before the end of the lesson. Make sure it is done properly by the end of the lesson otherwise you will have to carry on cleaning in your own time. I will be back to check in a few minutes.' Smile and walk away but make sure that you talk to other students or look busy etc. so that you cannot get involved in a further conversation with the students.

Finish the lesson in the usual orderly manner and start to dismiss the other students while walking over and checking that the graffiti has been cleaned off. Hopefully, the students will have done as you have requested. However, if they have not made any attempt to clean it then you will need to follow through with your threat that they will have to stay behind and clean it. You can tell them that they were warned and it needs to be done. Ignore any of their comments about being late for lessons, lunch, sport practice etc. Just keep repeating that the quicker they do it, the faster they will leave your room. One of the students will end up removing it even if it is not the one that you think is the culprit. Thank and praise the student for doing this and then dismiss them all. This should have solved the problem for this lesson but how does it prevent it from happening in the future?

Handling the situation with some humour in the next lesson can help to resolve the issue. At the start of the next lesson, give out pieces of blank paper to the students who were involved. Again, try not to single out any one student as this will lead to a confrontation. As you give out the paper say something along the lines of 'After last lesson, if the urge to write on the desks takes over again, I have given you some blank paper to use instead as I suggest you use the paper rather than the desk into the future.' This sends a strong message in a non-confrontational manner to the students that you are still aware of the issue and that you do not wish it to happen again. You might find that walking over to the students a couple of times during the lesson and saying 'Just checking that you are using the paper rather than the desk. Well done – for not using the desk' helps to reinforce your message. However, you will have to judge whether this might end up being seen as confrontational with these students.

EXTRA NOTE

If the graffiti is offensive about you or someone else in the class then you might need to take further action. The more tricky one to handle is if the graffiti is about you as the student knows you will read it and wants you to read it. Dealing with it in the classroom in front of everyone is not going to be the most successful approach. Sometimes, a flippant comment of 'Great – you have spelt all the words correctly' and then walking away can work. However, this won't solve the underlying problem but you can follow one of the above if you think the student will clean it off.

Another approach to consider would be to acknowledge that you have read it as you can show you are not embarrassed by it by making a comment as I have suggested or something similar. Do nothing else and end the lesson as usual. Once all the students have left the room, take a quick photo of it with your phone. Then quickly clean it off or move the desk somewhere else in the room or if you are really desperate (another class about to come in) stick down paper all over it and tell the next student that glue was split all over the desk and this was the best you can do.

As soon as you can during the day, go and talk to someone more senior about it. Show the photo to your Head of Department or someone else and ask about how you should proceed. You need to make sure that someone talks to the student before your next lesson with or without you there. The content of the graffiti will determine the action that is taken by other members of staff. However, within the context of your classroom you will have dealt with the incident in a clear, decisive and non-confrontational manner which will inevitably help to avoid it happening again.

A student hands in homework which is of poor quality

Please hand in your homework on your way out

You are collecting in homework at the end of the lesson. You have asked for the exercise book to be left open revealing the page showing this week's completed homework. As you are doing this, you notice that the homework of student A has not been done very well or in detail. You have talked to student A about this on two previous occasions and he/she has promised that it will improve. This is clearly not the case.

WHAT DO YOU DO NEXT?

1   In front of the class ask student A to stay behind and talk to you about the quality of their homework. Student A should stay behind but will their attitude towards you be more positive or negative since you have brought their lack of homework to the attention of the whole class? Would it be better to ask them to stay behind by talking to them one-to-one at their desk? Are you going to put them in detention for not doing their homework? Are you going to ask them about why they have not completed their homework? Are you going to tell them that you are disappointed about their lack of effort? Is this lack of effort representative of what they do in class? Is the lack of effort surprising to you? Do you think there could be other reasons why homework is not being completed? Do you need to ask this student whether there is something you can do to help them complete their homework?

2 Take in the homework and say nothing. However, as soon as possible go and talk to student A's form tutor/Head of Year/your Head of Department etc. and find out whether there is any further information you should know about this student. There may be reasons for this student not completing homework and you may find out that in other subjects they don't hand in any homework at all. Therefore, by handing in something to you this student has acknowledged the help that you have given them in the past, which might make you feel differently about the poor-quality homework. The information that you have gained about this student will then help you write an appropriate comment on the homework. This might be a more effective way of communicating with this student than talking to them about the situation.

Some students prefer to have a dialogue about their learning via written comments, written feedback or targets rather than verbal feedback in class or on a one-to-one basis. You may find that you can create a more reflective response to your comments on students' work if your comments are framed as questions rather than written as declarative statements about what you have read. For example, you could write (on a piece of English homework):

Well done [name of student]. I really like what you have written about the language of the poem.

- Why did you choose that specific metaphor to write about and not one of the others?
- How many other similes could you have written about?
- Can you identify one other language feature that you could have written about?

Writing the questions down in bullet point form then gives the students space to write down their answers to the questions. You need to give time for the students to do this when you hand back homework/work. One of the most depressing features of marking is to see the lack of time that students spend on reading your comments. Writing your comments as questions can help focus your feedback and encourage the students to engage with what you have written. You may find that you end up writing the same questions down on students' work, so writing some generic questions on the board that you want all (or a selection) of the students to answer about their homework/work can considerably help your marking load. At the same time, this will encourage a discussion with the students about the quality and learning that has taken place from the work they have completed.

3 Tell student A in front of the class that he/she is in detention (or whatever is appropriate for your school context) due to the lack of homework. Point out that this is not the first time that this has happened and that everyone else completes their homework to a reasonable standard and therefore student A will give up their own time to ensure that the homework is completed properly. Taking this approach clearly asserts your authority and shows the importance that you are place on homework. However, will putting student A in detention help to stop the lack of homework from happening again since this is not the first time?

Another issue to consider with detention is that it depends on how it is run in your school. Are detention sessions run by the class teacher or someone more senior? How are you going to ensure that the homework is completed properly during this session? Can you be sure that student A does understand the work? You need to be clear about your reasons for putting student A in detention – is it for a behaviour management reason or is it to help the learning of student A? If the lack of homework is connected with lack of general effort in class etc. then a detention may help. However, you might want to be more honest about the reasons for putting student A in detention and not let them and the rest of the class think that it is just about lack of effort in homework.

EXTRA NOTE

The context of dealing with student A is from the perspective that this is a student who works to a reasonable level in class and there are no regular incidences of poor behaviour from them.

However, you will need to deal differently with the lack of homework from a student who does not participate positively in your lessons, does not behave appropriately in your lessons and does not really complete work to a satisfactory standard. Finding out more information about these types of students will improve your confidence in dealing with them. Seek out their previous teachers in your subject and find out what techniques they used to obtain work/good behaviour from them. Talk to their form tutors/your Head of Department and find out what is going to be realistic for you to achieve with these students in your lesson. Finding out what is realistic does not mean that you should not set high expectations for all of your students. However, it does mean that you should have more information about the students before you start to implement practices (for example, immediate detentions for lack of homework) that will inevitably fail as you do not have the right support or knowledge about these students before you start.

A student turns off another's computer

It is towards the end of your lesson and the students have been working on computers. Student A leans across and turns off student B's computer and student B is now claiming that they have lost a lesson's work.

WHAT DO YOU DO?

1   Shout at student (A) and say 'Why did you do that? What was the point of doing that? What did that achieve? How are we going to get back student B's work? Are you going to redo it for them? Stay behind at the end of the lesson and we will talk about whether I am going to put you in detention/ talk to Head of Department etc. [whatever it is appropriate for your school context].'

Talking to student A in this manner will definitely put across your frustration at the situation and your disappointment with student A. The rest of the class will see your reaction and will know that this type of behaviour is not appropriate. However, how does it solve student B's problem? Who gains from your shouting? Does shouting make your frustration any clearer? Could it escalate the situation? Is student A likely to behave negatively at this point? Could you end up dealing with a further behaviour management issue from student A? What has it done to the atmosphere of your lesson? Are you still able to finish your lesson in an orderly and reflective manner? If you finish the lesson in this manner, you may find that the main event that the students will remember from your lesson is of you shouting.

2   Move close to student A and quickly tell them in a calm and measured tone that their behaviour has been inappropriate and they need to stay behind at the end of the lesson. Then move to student B and explain how the IT technicians will probably be able to find a copy of the document on the network. Ask whether they saved their work at all during the lesson. If not, this might cause more of a problem but still reassure student B that it can be solved. At this point, have you disrupted the other students? You have also quickly intervened with both students. You will still have time to continue with your lesson and ensure that it ends in an orderly and reflective manner. You must make sure that student A stays behind at the end of the lesson as they will probably try to sneak out. When you talk to them at the end of the lesson, you need to give out the sanctions that you think are appropriate depending on your school context. If this is not the first time this has happened you might need to escalate it further.

3   Tell student A to leave the classroom immediately and wait outside for you. You can then talk to student B and suggest some measures that can be taken. For example, you will talk to the IT technicians and see if they can find it on the network etc. You should also try to emphasise how important it is to save work regularly when working on computers. In future lessons, you might want to stop the lesson at appropriate moments and insist that everyone saves their work. Students seem to have a tendency to forget to save their work on a regular basis and then become very upset when they lose it.

You may also take this opportunity to see if you can establish why you think student A turned off student's B computer. Is this something that has happened before between them? Should they not sit near to each other in the future?

You could also try and establish exactly how much work student B had completed. Sometimes, students appear very upset about the work they have lost but then you find out that they had only written four lines. They can use this type of incident to gain attention from you and also to ensure that student A gets into trouble by exaggerating the amount of work they have lost.

If you have time in the lesson, you can ask student B to dictate their work to another student who can type it on the computer for them. Student B could also try to quickly write down what they had typed. The student might claim that they cannot remember but ask them to be positive and it doesn't matter if they don't write down every word. Sometimes, telling them that student A will have to type out whatever they have remembered tends to help their memory.

You can then finish your lesson in an orderly and reflective manner and wait for the students to leave. Then tell student A to come back into the classroom. Talk to them in a quiet and controlled manner and explain what the sanction will be for their behaviour. You may also wish to see if you can find out why they felt this was appropriate behaviour. Had they thought through what would happen afterwards? Try and see if you can create some empathy with the feelings that student B had felt after the incident. Be very clear about what will happen in future lessons (not sit near student B etc.) and when/where they will have their detention etc. Try and finish the conversation on a positive note, especially if student A has handled this conversation with you in an appropriate manner. This might help to ensure that they attend their detention (or other sanction) and you are less likely to have any behaviour management problems from student A at the start of the next lesson.

CHAPTER *4*

MANAGING THE BEHAVIOUR OF STUDENTS AS THEY LEAVE YOUR CLASSROOM

What do you do when a student . . .

SCENARIO *1*

A student leaves the classroom before you have dismissed the class

A student leaves the classroom before you have dismissed the class. Student A gets up from his/her chair and walks out instead of waiting for you to tell the students that they can leave.

WHAT DO YOU DO NEXT?

1 Make some comment about student A's early departure and then say 'Well, [name of student] has clearly gone so you might as well all go too. You have worked well today so that is why I am letting you go a few minutes early – well done. See you next lesson.'

By doing this, you are attempting to turn a negative into a positive by rewarding the students who have stayed behind. You are suggesting that student A leaving early is not such a big thing which is why you are letting the rest of the students go too. The students will be pleased with your response and probably leave saying 'Thanks Sir/Miss.' However, what has it shown about who is in control of your lesson even at the end? Is it you or is it student A? You may have had a tough lesson and you are pleased to see the back of student A and most of the other students too but what is going to happen next lesson? Will the students keep asking if they can go early again? Will student A leave early again if he/she thinks that it will help his/her classmates? How are you going to reinstate a routine to dismiss the class? Will the students try to alter some of your other routines in the class if they see that you can give in so easily? Ultimately, the students will know that you have been pleased to see them leave early and will probably aim to make you do it again in future lessons so an incident that seems quite small can lead to further behaviour management problems.

2   Walk to the door and tell student A to return. The likelihood is that they will not return at this stage. What is happening to the rest of the class at this point? Will it be easy to return and to dismiss the other students in an orderly fashion? Will some of the students try to leave when they have seen one of their classmates do the same? How are you going to stop them from leaving if your attention is on student A who is walking away from you down the corridor? Why do you think student A felt that he/she could behave in this way? Was there too much time between packing up and dismissing the class? Were the students getting bored? Did you get distracted by doing something else instead of focusing on dismissing the class? Do you have clear guidelines about how you want to finish your lesson and use them consistently?

3   Praise the students who are still in the class and say something along the lines of 'Right, well done for ignoring the behaviour of [name of student]. You have all worked really well today and I look forward to working with you in the next lesson.' Then dismiss the class in the usual way. It is important that you praise the behaviour of the students who are demonstrating good behaviour but you need to acknowledge the poor behaviour of student A. You should not pretend that it has not happened as the students will be interested in seeing your reaction. You might want to add a comment that student A will clearly be completing a detention or whatever is appropriate for your school context. This will demonstrate to the students that there are clear consequences to poor behaviour in your lesson.

If you think there is any chance that student A is not going to attend their next lesson or that they will leave the school site, you need to let someone know before you start your next lesson. The School Office might be the first place to contact and let them know what has happened so that they can inform an appropriate person to check on the whereabouts of student A.

Before you have another lesson with student A you need to talk to someone else about their behaviour. This might be student A's form tutor, your Head of Department etc. You need to take advice on whether this is a common occurrence or whether there was something specific that might have triggered student A's response. This information will then guide you about how you are going to handle the conversation you need to have with student A. You might need to find them at break time, lunchtime, during registration etc. but you need to have a quick chat with the student about their behaviour at the end of your lesson before they return. You need to be firm about your expectations but you also need to be confident that you are able to implement these expectations with the class and this student.

For example, insisting that a class is dismissed in silence can be an ideal situation but one that you might not be able to implement from the start until you have a better working relationship with a class. You need to be realistic about what you can enforce without creating confrontations between yourself and the students. It may be that students having chairs tucked in, facing the front and then leaving on a signal from you is enough with some classes. You may know of other teachers who have their classes in silence before the students are dismissed, but do not worry about this. Simply ensure that you have a formal routine that you use every lesson in order to dismiss the class but make sure it is a realistic one for the context of the class you are dealing with. You have to be able to ensure that the same routine is done every single lesson, so it has to be obtainable, otherwise your lessons will always end in a negative manner.

Your students seem to leave your classroom very noisily

Your students seem to leave your classroom very noisily. After you have dismissed the students there is a rugby scrum for the door with students shouting and shoving each other. It only lasts for a minute but another member of staff has commented to you about how eager your students seem to be to leave your lessons.

HOW CAN YOU IMPROVE THE SITUATION?

1   You can dismiss students table by table, row by row etc. You can do this by asking the students questions about the lesson and when they have answered them correctly, they can leave the classroom. This takes preparation as you can end up asking the same questions or simple recall questions such as 'What was the name of the process that we learnt in today's lesson?' If these questions are going to act as your plenary then they will need to be more thought provoking. You can ask the students to pack up and stand behind their desks and then ask the questions.

However, the students can become quite restless and are not really doing any thinking at this point unless you have organised enough time for this activity. Inevitably the bell will go when you are halfway through this activity and that is fine for the students who have already gone but if you have still another fifteen students to ask, this can become a laborious and counter-productive way of ending the lesson. It tends to mean that you ask another three to four students and then say to the others 'Well done, you have worked well and you can leave now.' Inevitably, it means that you have not checked that all students have understood the learning, and how are you going to ensure that this doesn't happen to the same students in the next lesson?

Releasing the students in this manner will have controlled their exit from your classroom but will they have actually learnt anything in the process? This can be a successful method if your questions are prepared in advance, targeted at specific students and given enough time at the end of the lesson. However, do not over-use this method as it does not really allow much time for reflection about future learning. The discussions can be quite forced, especially if the students have already packed up as everyone's eye is inevitably on the door.

2 You can ask students to complete an activity which requires them to give you something as they leave the classroom. This then controls the flow of students leaving your classroom. Writing on a post-it note which they leave on a board/table/sugar paper can work quite well. You can ask them to write on the post-it note what they have learnt during the lesson/a question they would like answered in the next lesson/the answer to the key questions for today's lesson/give themselves a level for effort/understanding/the definition of a key word from the lesson etc.

You could also ask the students to hand in their homework at the front of the classroom as they leave. You can ask them to put their homework/classwork in specific coloured boxes depending on their level of understanding. For example, you could have red, yellow and green boxes at the front of the class. The students then place their homework in the right box: red = didn't really understand the homework; yellow = my understanding was OK; green = didn't have any problems with homework. This strategy of using boxes for students to place work in can be extended to level of effort, answers to key questions etc. Even at this final stage of the lesson it is still encouraging the students to be reflective about their work and it can lead to further discussion at the start of the next lesson as you can ask students to justify their choices. For example, with homework you will inevitably find students who have either under-estimated or over-estimated their understanding of the homework and this can lead to interesting individual conversations during the next lesson about the reasons for their choices.

3 Move a few paces away from the door of your classroom and dismiss the students from there. Ensure that each student walks past you and make some comment about their behaviour/attitude/work ethic in that lesson that is specific to them. Initially the students will walk past you at their usual speed but you are still there to control the flow and noise as they leave the room. However, over a short period of time you will find that students will slow down as they walk past you in order to hear what you are going to say about them. This can work well with difficult classes as generic praise is not very motivating for certain students but they respond really well to individual praise if it is relevant, specific and appropriate to them.

A student regularly stays behind to talk to you

Once you have dismissed the class, a student regularly stays behind and wants to talk to you. They want to talk about the lesson but they also want to tell you about what they like doing but also find out more details about you too. This is now the third lesson that the student has stayed behind to talk to you.

HOW DO YOU HANDLE THIS SITUATION?

1 If the student is stopping you from clearing up, organising your materials for next lesson or grabbing a quick coffee before the start of the next lesson, you need to be honest about this. You need to tell the student that if they want to talk to you about your lesson then maybe they should come back at the end of school and you can meet in the library. Try not to encourage a discussion at lunchtime as certain students would rather spend their lunchtimes with members of staff than their peers. If you think this student would benefit from having your classroom as a safe haven then it can be a situation that you can work out. However, it has to be on the ground rules that you can get on with your work; it will also depend on the context of your school, as students are sometimes not allowed in classrooms at lunchtimes etc.

You might want to check with this student's form tutor about organising this arrangement as it might cause you problems if you wish to have meetings with other students or make phone calls etc. in your classroom. You may want to find out if there are other 'safe havens' in the school that this student can use. Some students like to latch onto a new teacher as they feel that it is easier to obtain attention from a teacher who is trying to make a good impression in the school.

2 Tell the student that you are happy to talk to them about your lesson after school or at lunchtime but consider whether you should have any other conversation with their form tutor. You need to be clear about your role with this student _ are you their subject teacher or do you have a pastoral role with them? As a new teacher to the school it is probably best to leave the pastoral aspect to more experienced teachers unless you have been given specific guidance about how to deal with this student. Combining the subject role with a pastoral role with certain students (who are not in your tutor group) can be one of the most draining aspects of the job. You need to be quite clear with students that you need time to do some of the things that your job demands of you. There are other staff that students can talk to and you need to find out who these are so you can recommend this course of action to them.

3 You need to maintain the student/teacher distance with students, especially in the early days, and not disclose too much personal information about yourself. Do not be concerned about discouraging the student from spending too much time with you, especially if you have given him/her other alternatives. One of the most rewarding parts of teaching is spending time with young people and offering them guidance and support. However, there is a line that defines when these types of discussion can happen, how long they should be for, where they should happen and who should be involved in them. You will need to refer to the safeguarding policy of your school for further detailed guidance about how to handle these types of situation. Essentially, you need to look after your own well-being by not spending too much time with one student if it starts to impact on the time, preparation and energy that you have for all the other students you teach.

CHAPTER 5

MANAGING THE BEHAVIOUR OF STUDENTS IN THE CORRIDOR

What do you do when a student . . .

Incorrect school uniform

You are walking to your lesson, which is going to start in about five minutes, and you spot some students in the corridor waiting outside another classroom,who are not wearing the correct uniform. Depending on your school that could be: their shirt is untucked, they are wearing trainers, they are still wearing a coat etc.

WHAT DO YOU DO?

1   Ignore the students as their form tutor should have asked them about their lack of uniform or their class teacher will deal with it when they arrive. You have your class to get to and you feel that you are enforcing the school uniform policy by ensuring that the students you teach are wearing the correct uniform.

2   You challenge the students with 'Why are you wearing trainers? Who said you could wear trainers? You know that this is against the school rules, you need to change them immediately.' What is going to be the students' reaction to your challenge? What are you going to do if they don't change their trainers? What type of excuse are they going to give you about wearing trainers? What do you do if they don't comply? What kind of sanctions can you impose at this stage when you are on the way to your lesson?

You need to extract yourself from this situation as quickly as possible if the students become confrontational, and tell them that you will see them later. Do not ask for their names as they won't give them to you. Carry on to your class and teach your lesson. At the end of the lesson, go and find the class teacher and tell them what has happened. Ask to see the photos of the students in the class list – most schools have photos of their students in class lists. Find out the names of the students and with some guidance from the class teacher, go and find these students and talk to them about their inappropriate behaviour in the corridor. If you can do this in the same day then it is liable to be more effective. Try to talk to the students away from their mates, do not talk to them while they are sitting in a group somewhere, talk to them individually.

You have then followed up the incident at an appropriate time for you and the students will know that there is a consequence to their actions. Next time you walk past these students and ask them to sort out their uniform, you have significantly improved the chances of them doing it.

3 Walk up to the students and say 'You know that you are not meant to be wearing trainers. Why are you wearing them? If you have got your other shoes here, I suggest you change them before your class teacher arrives. Can you make sure that I don't see you in trainers again?' You can then choose to walk away (so you are not late for your lesson) or stay for their response if you think it is appropriate.

If you follow this approach, how are the students going to react to this challenge? Are you demanding instant action? It shouldn't take up too much of your time. By doing this you are letting them know that you have noticed their lack of conformity and you are supporting the school's policy on enforcing the correct uniform. How does this help your status as a teacher? You are sending a clear message to students about your standards and that you support the expectations of the school. This will help you in the future if you end up teaching these students. Additionally, it sends the message to students that all staff have the same expectations and will enforce them. Ultimately, a consistent approach being adopted by all staff to issues such as lack of uniform, poor punctuality, bad behaviour etc. is one of the ways that changes can be made to the attitudes of students.

EXTRA NOTE

If you receive a negative reaction from the students to (3) which is a low-level way of dealing with the situation, you may wish to mention it to their class teacher at some point during the day or before their next lesson. Ask to see a photo class list of the students and go and talk to the students who were involved. Alternatively, you can deal with it again when you see the same group of students at the start of another lesson (outside the same classroom) as this time you will know their names. Simply being able to use a student's name can have a significant impact on their behaviour as it suggests to them that you have knowledge about them and are therefore more likely to act on their poor behaviour.

SCENARIO 2

Students drop litter in the corridor

You are walking to your classroom at the end of lunchtime and you see two students, whom you know, drop litter in the corridor ahead of you.

WHAT DO YOU DO?

1   You shout the names of the students and say to them 'You have just dropped that litter on the floor and you need to pick it up and put it in the bin.' Their reaction is likely to be 'It wasn't us, we didn't drop the litter so we are not picking it up.' What do you do now to avoid the confrontation? How are you going to make them pick up the litter when they are refusing to do so?

2   You shout the names of the students to attract their attention and then walk up to them. '[Names of students] I saw you two drop some litter in the corridor and you know that dropping litter is breaking one of our school rules. If we let everyone drop litter all the time, we wouldn't all be able to learn in a clean and healthy environment would we? It would be great if you could do your bit and pick up your litter and find a bin. Thanks.' You then walk away quite quickly and only turn back towards them after a few steps to check that they have done it.

CHAPTER 5: *Managing students in the corridor*   **123**

With this approach, you are explaining the reason why the students are not meant to drop litter and you are giving them a reason for picking up their litter. Note that you have not used 'please' but 'thanks'. It is not a request so you have not used 'please' but you are saying 'thanks' to model good manners. Using 'thanks' in this way also suggests that you are expecting the students to comply. You are not turning it into a confrontation as you are walking away and technically giving them a choice to follow your instructions or not.

3   You pick up the litter and walk up to them both and say 'I believe this is your litter. Can you find a bin to put it into? You know that you are not meant to drop litter. Thanks.' You then walk away but check after a few steps that they have done what you have asked.

Again, you are avoiding a confrontation as you are walking away which is suggesting you are expecting their compliance. You have modelled the correct behaviour by picking up the litter in the first place. You have also not used 'please' so it is not a request and you have indicated that you are expecting them to comply by saying 'thanks'.

SCENARIO *3*

Play fighting in the corridor

You are on your way to your lesson at the end of break and are aware that your class may be waiting for you. You come across three students pushing each other in the corridor, it is play fighting. They stop as you make eye contact with them but start again as soon as you walk past.

WHAT DO YOU DO?

1 Turn round and shout 'What are you doing? That is not an appropriate type of behaviour in the corridor. What are your names? I expect to see you at the end of the lesson outside my classroom.'

How are the students going to react to this? Are you going to have their cooperation? What are you going to do if they don't give you their names or run off? Have you got time to find them? What are you going to do if they don't come at the end of your lesson? How are you going to know that they have given you their real names? What are the other students doing in the corridor while this is going on? How much time has this taken up?

2 Turn round and say to them 'That type of behaviour is not appropriate in the corridor as you might hurt someone and yourselves. What is the name of your class teacher? Right, I suggest that you stop otherwise I will have to tell your class teacher about your inappropriate behaviour.'

With this approach you have identified the reason why they should stop their behaviour and you have commented on their behaviour and not on them as individuals. You have also given them a choice to stop it or otherwise you will tell their class teacher. You don't have to ask those particular students for the name of the teacher, another student standing in the corridor will tell you if you don't know already. You can then walk away but glance back over your shoulder so the students know you are still watching them. What do the students now realise about your attitude towards behaviour in the school?

You could also mention this very minor incident concerning behaviour outside the classroom to the class teacher at some point that day. You could ask the class teacher to mention to their students that you had talked to them about it. This will also help to reinforce to the students that you follow up bad behaviour. If you do these things you will find there is probably a change in the behaviour of the same students when you walk past them in the corridor at a future point.

3   Carry on walking as if it wasn't anything serious. You know one of the students involved and you are confident that he wouldn't do anything too bad. Also, the bell has just rung and you are sure that the usual class teacher will be there in a minute. However, will these students stop if the same thing happens tomorrow, when you walk past? What will these students think about your approach to behaviour in the school? Will they think that every member of staff takes poor behaviour seriously?

A student is banging their head

You are walking in the corridor towards your classroom as it is about five minutes from the start of your lesson. You come across a student (that you don't know) who is banging their head against the wall.

WHAT DO YOU DO?

1 You can walk past and immediately alert another appropriate member of staff. This means that you have passed the situation on to another member of staff who is probably more experienced in dealing with this type of situation. However, you may feel that you should return to the corridor and monitor the situation if there is a time delay in this member of staff arriving. You may wish to read (3) to help you work out how to talk to the student while you are waiting for assistance.

2 You can walk up close to the student and ask them to stop it as they could hurt themselves. This does not always work and the student may ignore you. Other students may tell you that this student is doing it for attention and it happens regularly. This does not mean that you should not take it seriously and find another more experienced member of staff. You will find that once you get involved it is likely to be given more attention by other students so you may wish to refer to (3).

3   Immediately ask a student who is nearby to go to the School Office/
Reception/senior staff etc. and tell them that you need assistance
immediately. Stand close to the student and ask them to stop what they are
doing as they could hurt themselves. Start talking to the student about the
reasons why they are doing this. Ask the student if there is something that
they would like you to do? For example, is there a member of staff they
would like you to get? Would they like you to do something? The student
may stop banging their head in order to answer your questions.

While talking to the student, keep your voice calm with a 'chatty' tone to it.
This is not only for the benefit of the student but for the others around you.
You can suggest on a personal level why you would like the student to stop
thumping their head. Sometimes, humour may help at this point but it
depends on the context and how serious you think the situation has become.

EXTRA NOTE

By the time you have completed (3) you would hope that another member of staff
will have arrived to assist you. This takes the pressure and responsibility off you and
gives you support in handling the situation in an appropriate manner within the
context of your school and the student. You should not feel that you need to deal
with this situation by yourself. It is always one where you should get other staff
involved as soon as possible.

SCENARIO 5

My friend thinks you are fit

You are walking down a corridor and a teenage student stops you to say 'My best friend thinks you are well fit' (this is the first time that this has been said to you by this student).

WHAT CAN YOU DO?

1 Look shocked and rush away. What do you think is going to be the reaction of the student? The student is going to realise that you are embarrassed and will gain some satisfaction from this. How are you going to handle the situation when the student enters your classroom the next day and says 'Miss/Sir, are you embarrassed that my mate thinks you are fit?' What will you be able to say at this point?

2 Challenge the student by saying 'That sort of comment is inappropriate and I don't wish to hear you use that type of language again.' What is the student going to say to that? Think about where you are saying this – it is in the corridor. Are other students going to be listening? What is the student going to say next 'Miss/Sir, calm down, I was only having a laugh. Does that mean you fancy him/her too?' How are you going to handle this or similar comments if the situation escalates in any way in the corridor? What is going to be your next comment to this student? What is going to be the student's reply?

3 Smile, make some sarcastic comment and carry on walking. The sarcastic comment could be along the lines of 'How amazing – to have such attention at my age. See you next lesson.' How is the student going to react now? Have you escalated it in any way? Who has had the last word? Does the student have anything to say about this when he sees you in the next lesson? With this type of comment, you have also emphasised the age difference which is reinforcing the point about the distance that will be maintained between you and your students.

EXTRA NOTE

If these comments are repeated by the same student/s at any other time then different action might need to be taken. You will need to talk to your Head of Department or another experienced teacher to find out if embarrassing new teachers is something that this student does on a regular basis. You might need to take advice from other teachers in your school about how to handle the comments, especially if they are repeated in front of the whole class.

Index

offensive graffiti 101

Ofsted ix

one-to-one conversations: in corridor 3, 7, 8, 9, 16, 30, 44, 78; at end of lesson 3, 91, 94–5; at student's desk 3, 26, 73, 77, 102

organisational skills 10

parents: letters from 15–19; letters to 14

partners, learning and talk 33, 35, 72

pastoral role 117; see also form tutors

peer teaching 84–5, 87

'pens down and facing the front' culture 81

pen tapping 57–8

photographs: in class list 121, 122; of graffiti 101

physical presence, use of 21, 33, 66, 80

physical restraint 20

'picked on' complaints 22, 24–5, 76–9

play fighting 125–6

please, use of term 24–5, 32–3, 57, 82, 124

policies see school policies and rules

positive relationships, maintaining 53, 74

praise: during continuous monitoring 25, 26, 30, 52; of group 71–2, 90–1; individual versus generic 115; rewarding positive behaviour 8, 26, 78, 79, 91, 111; for work after poor behaviour 29, 31, 48, 74

presentations 85–6, 90–2

quizzes 85

reasons for behaviour: asking for in writing 3–4, 5; asking students to explain 23, 30, 41, 46, 77, 94; finding out from colleagues 12, 75, 103, 105

reasons for rules, explaining 5, 41–2, 49–50, 123–4, 125–6

Reception see School Office

recurring behaviour: asking for toilet breaks 6–9; forgetting equipment 10–12; lateness 14

refusing to work: in a group 70–2; in lessons 51–3; with teaching assistants 27–31

removal from lessons 28, 62, 75, 95; see also sending students out

rewarding behaviour see praise

routines, use of 36, 111, 112

ruining another's work 93–7, 106–8

rules see school policies and rules

safeguarding policies 117

safety issues 20–1, 61, 127–8

sanctions: escalation of 52, 79; threats of 21, 52, 80, 83; use of 63, 66, 71, 75, 95, 108; see also detention

sarcasm 2, 82, 90, 130

School Office: informing about missing students 61, 111; letters from parents 16–17, 18, 19; requesting assistance from 64, 128

school policies and rules: explaining reasons for 5, 41–2, 123–4; on homophobic language 69; invoking 40, 50, 59, 60, 63; on leaving school premises 17; safeguarding policies 117; on uniforms 120, 121

school premises, leaving 15–19, 111

seating plans 32–5, 72, 84–5

sending students out: avoiding 55; for inappropriate behaviour towards other students 65–6, 93–4, 96, 107; for inappropriate behaviour towards teacher 42, 72, 75, 76–7, 78; leaving when sent out 61–4; for poor behaviour 11, 13–14, 74; when situations escalate 28, 52, 71, 78

senior colleagues: reporting issues to 31, 61, 63, 67–8, 99, 101; support from 62, 63, 75; see also Head of Department; Head of Year

shouting: avoiding 18, 75, 94, 99; by students 62, 93, 95, 113; at students in class 20, 43, 74, 78, 81, 106–7; at students in corridor 123, 125

signing out policies 17

silence, trying to enforce 37, 112